PROPHETIC STRAIN

PROPHETIC STRAIN

The Greater Lyric in the Eighteenth Century

ANNE WILLIAMS

THE UNIVERSITY OF CHICAGO PRESS

Chicago & London

ANNE WILLIAMS is assistant professor of English
at the University of Georgia.

THE UNIVERSITY OF CHICAGO PRESS, CHICAGO 60637
THE UNIVERSITY OF CHICAGO PRESS, LTD., LONDON
© 1984 by The University of Chicago
All rights reserved. Published 1984
Printed in the United States of America
93 92 91 90 89 88 87 86 85 84   5 4 3 2 1

LIBRARY OF CONGRESS CATALOGING IN PUBLICATION DATA

Williams, Anne.
    Prophetic strain.

    Includes bibliographical references and index.
    1. English poetry—18th century—History and criticism.
2. Lyric poetry—History and criticism. 3. Romanticism—
England. 4. Odes—History and criticism. I. Title.
PR551.W48 1984   821'.04'09   83-24103
ISBN 0-226-89916-0
ISBN 0-226-89917-9 (pbk.)

To John

And may at last my weary age
Find out the peaceful hermitage,
The Hairy Gown and Mossy Cell,
Where I may sit and rightly spell
Of every Star that Heav'n doth shew
And every Herb that sips the dew;
Till old experience do attain
To something like Prophetic strain.

John Milton
"Il Penseroso"

Contents

Acknowledgments

Perhaps every female scholar considers at some time or other the analogies between writing a book and having a baby. During the years that I labored over this manuscript, however, I have more often pondered the medieval legend that infant bears are born as amorphous lumps of flesh which the mother, during her long hibernation, prods and pummels into proper bear shape. While struggling to form masses of historical, theoretical, and poetic matter into a coherent book, I have felt deep sympathies for her endeavor.

This study began as research into the history of ideas, an attempt to trace the intellectual background of Wordsworth's "theodicy of the landscape" as set forth in *The Prelude*. I wish to thank Professor M. H. Abrams, who supervised the original thesis, for his encouragement at that time, and most especially for the inordinate number of letters of recommendation I have since requested.

The National Endowment for the Humanities supported this project on two occasions. During the summer of 1976 I was privileged to attend a seminar at Brown University directed by Professors Barbara K. Lewalski and Mason Lowance. The topic was "The Puritan Imagination in England and America, 1590–1776." In reading a good deal of Renaissance Protestant theology and poetry, I was excited to discover such supposedly Romantic and Wordsworthian notions as "creative perception" and the spiritual value of nature already prevalent in theory and practice. By the end of that summer I had a book with a beginning and an end, but no middle, and a great many answers to questions I could not as yet articulate.

Only in 1977, four years after the original thesis had been completed, did the right questions seem to present themselves.

I spent 1977–78 at Boston University as an NEH Fellow-in-Residence, studying English and American lyric poetry with Professor Helen Vendler, whose stimulating example as a reader of poetry enabled me to see my material from an entirely different angle. It occurred to me that the link I sought between the seventeenth century and the nineteenth lay not in the continuity of subject—poetry about nature—but in the peculiar poetic metamorphosis that had apparently occurred during the eighteenth century: how had small lyrics grown into such large ones? How, in fact, had the lyric usurped the realm of verse?

I wish to thank both Professor Lewalski and Professor Vendler also for subsequently reading portions of the manuscript and making helpful suggestions. The following friends and colleagues at Georgia have generously given of their time to read or proofread: Rosemary Franklin, Coburn Freer, Charles I. Patterson, Jr., Frances Teague, and Frank Warnke. I am grateful to my department for a research grant in the summer of 1980, for extensive secretarial help, and for the aid of a graduate assistant, John Davis, who patiently checked all my footnotes. I also wish to thank the editors of *Romanticism Past and Present* for permission to reprint, from volume 5, no. 1, of that journal, the analysis of Wordsworth's *Intimations Ode* (now chapter 9) which they published, in somewhat different form.

My greatest debt, however, is acknowledged in the dedication of this book to my husband, John D. Boyd. He listened, encouraged, edited—and not least, admits no impediment to the marriage of two careers one thousand miles apart.

Prologue

In late seventeenth-century discussions, the term "greater lyric" was a synonym for "ode." Such poems were greater not so much in size as in purpose, their special preserve being the high themes of praise and prayer. With the important exception of the ode, however, the lyric was regarded as a minor genre, since it was brief, limited in scope, and devoted primarily to the expression of private experience. The English poetic tradition was rich in lyrics, but before about 1700 the majority of these were "songs and sonnets": poems often delightful but never to be thought commensurate in importance with the epics and tragedies honored by both classical and Renaissance tradition. The remaining minority were mostly odes—such as Milton's "On the Morning of Christ's Nativity" or Dryden's "Alexander's Feast"—poems conventionally diverse in their subjects but revealing an emotional range more or less limited to invocation and exaltation.

During the course of the eighteenth century, however, something revolutionary happened to English poetry. With surprising speed and thoroughness, the lyric usurped the realm of verse. Well before 1800, consequently, readers of modern poems would have been more surprised to encounter a work *not* essentially lyric in nature than one which was. (Just what I mean by "essentially lyric" will be the main concern of chapter 1.) In literary criticism this revolutionary change is usually said to be marked by Wordsworth's famous description of poetry (published in 1800) as "the spontaneous overflow of powerful feelings"; but by then lyrics had become various and flexible enough to accomplish all those functions of poetry which earlier had belonged to the narrative and dramatic modes—to epic, tragedy, satire, pastoral, or elegy. Between 1799 and 1805 Wordsworth wrote his version of epic, a work best understood as an anomalous

lyric-epic, *The Prelude;* he also wrote "tragedies," but they were
essentially lyrical-pastoral tragedies such as *The Ruined Cottage*
and "Michael."

Such clumsy ways of referring to these curious generic hybrids
seem necessary, though reminiscent of Polonius with his talk of
"pastoral-comical, historical-pastoral, tragical-pastorical, tragi-
cal-historical pastoral." Thus for my purpose in this book, I shall
revive the term "greater lyric" as the most convenient way of
designating the poems I discuss. By this term I shall refer not
only to the ode, or to a lyric merely longer than usual. I mean
by "greater lyric" a poem large in other dimensions as well: one
that concerns the abiding issues about man, nature, and human
life which have always occupied serious poets in their most ambitious work.

The central questions I shall explore concerning the unprecedented rise of the lyric and the concurrent development of
Romanticism throughout the eighteenth century might be "an-
swered" in any number of ways; indeed they have been, and
doubtless I owe more than I am fully aware to such works as
Abrams's *The Mirror and the Lamp* and *Natural Supernaturalism,*
to Monk's *The Sublime,* to Nicolson's *Mountain Gloom and Mountain
Glory,* or Tuveson's *The Imagination as a Means of Grace.* No one,
however, has sought to understand the realignment of poetry
that helps define the emergence of Romanticism by concentrat-
ing on developments in literary practice and experimentation,
that is, by viewing these broad literary changes from within the
poetry itself. One reason for this neglect, perhaps, is that the
perspectives traditionally offered by literary history have notoriously failed to disclose a coherent poetic tradition among the
major poems of the eighteenth century. Although the commonplace notion that Romanticism was a revolution has been so much
revised as to be nearly discredited in some quarters, an attempt
today to emphasize the continuities, rather than the radical dis-
junctions, between Pope and Wordsworth remains somewhat
anomalous.

The main principle of continuity shaping a tradition throughout the century preceding Wordsworth is, as I shall demonstrate,
that most of the popular and influential verse belongs to the
category of "greater lyric" as I have defined it. Thus my readers
will find here no discussions of the works usually taken to be

peculiarly eighteenth-century lyric types; no odes by Collins and
Gray. With the exception of Wordsworth's *Intimations Ode*, I have
avoided poems which obviously announce themselves as lyric. I
hope to show that the forces which led to the lyric's predominance before the end of the century are not manifested mainly
in song and sonnet, or only in the numerous "pindaricks" and
other similar poems so earnestly and numerously composed
throughout the century. In short, the central paradox implicit
in this survey is that the most intriguing and "prophetic strains"
of lyric appear in the great works traditionally regarded as characteristic "Augustan" or neoclassical art: Pope's *Eloisa to Abelard*,
Johnson's *Vanity of Human Wishes*, Gray's *Elegy*, Goldsmith's *Deserted Village*. (This book will persist in explicating the several
senses which this context may enable us to find in that Miltonic
phrase, "prophetic strain.") I have also omitted Blake, Smart,
and some other poets who might seem to help demonstrate my
hypothesis, since they were not immediately absorbed into the
tradition; I have limited my discussion to poems which were at
the time widely read and often quoted, the poetic favorites of
the century.

This strain of lyric in larger poems ostensibly (and, in part,
truly) belonging to other genres—epic, satire, elegy, epistle—
creates tensions which seem to me definitively characteristic of
the eighteenth-century greater lyric. When examined in a generic context, some of the most familiar works, such as Gray's
Elegy, reveal their distinctive powers through their oddly mixed
forms; they are hybrids which curiously unite public rhetoric
and private meditation, which successfully wed the lyric mode
to various nonlyric conventions. Since there was no convenient,
familiar vocabulary in which to talk about such strains, I have
begun, in the following chapter, with some speculations about
the nature of lyric itself. I hold to the premise that a useful
distinction can always be made between "mode" (meaning roughly
Aristotle's "manner of imitation") and "genre," which I define
as *any* perceived category of qualities, whether formal, conventional, or thematic, which reveals critically significant analogies
within a set of works. However closely any conventional genre
may be associated with a particular mode (as the sonnet is attached to the lyric), it may on occasion be attracted by others.
An overriding characteristic of the poems I shall discuss is that

they all reveal signs of such "generic appropriation"; various traditionally nonlyric genres are drawn by the magnetism of a newly powerful lyric mode.

Wordsworth comes at the conclusion of this discussion for a number of reasons. Because he has so often been thought of as a prototype and initiator of Romanticism, it is instructive to see in his poetry the fulfillment of a previous tradition, an end as well as a beginning. While much of Wordsworth's poetry epitomizes the quasi-autobiographical kind of poem which was to become our modern paradigm for the lyric, his larger works always show the same kinds of generic hybridization apparent in the poems of his immediate predecessors. Moreover, Wordsworth most clearly and self-consciously realizes those goals for the "restoration" of poetry which had already been established by the beginning of the eighteenth century.

From this historical perspective, I believe, the Romanticism of Wordsworth emphatically belongs to a native English tradition, one not usually acknowledged to exist in its own right. The poetry of eighteenth-century England can be seen as forming a genuine tradition in itself, rather than as a mere tangled web of "neoclassicism," "sensibility," and "preromanticism." Its principle of development, I suggest, is best described as continual generic experimentation accompanying the rise of the lyric throughout the century. Reading the poetry of the period in this light gives one a new sense of the accomplishment and the distinctive importance of its masterpieces. Eighteenth-century verse *is* transitional, as has always been assumed, but its highly distinctive lyrical strains prophesy what is to come, and strain toward the mode Wordsworth appropriated to himself: the prophetic.

PART ONE

Lyric Explorations

I

What Is the Lyric?

Practical criticism of the lyric—rich and varied as it has become—
sometimes recalls one implication of the Sapir-Whorf hypothesis:
we may ignore certain dimensions of lyric poetry because we
have no vocabulary to discuss them. Such blindness has a clear
historical cause. Ever since the late eighteenth century and the
full flowering of Romanticism, our view of poetry as a whole has
been focused on the lyric poem, and specifically focused on the
Romantic kind of lyric. Partly because that period produced so
many deservedly celebrated lyrics, and partly because of the
influence of such Romantic theorists as Coleridge, Mill, Wordsworth, and Poe, most readers for the past century or so have
not only regarded the lyric as the poem par excellence, but have
tacitly defined poetry as lyric poetry.

Hence "lyric" (now frequently synonymous with "short poem")
is one of our most familiar terms, yet remains a singularly unex-
amined one. The standard definitions of lyric reflect Romantic
theory and Romantic practice almost exclusively, though we may
sometimes reassert the more primitive associations of the lyric
with music. "A lyric," according to one such definition, "is a brief
subjective poem strongly marked by imagination, melody, and
emotion, and creating for the reader a single, unified impression." Another defines it as "any fairly short, nonnarrative poem
presenting a single speaker who expresses a state of mind or a
process of thought and feeling." C. Day Lewis (in a somewhat
idiosyncratic strain) insists that the form is so closely allied with
music that only the poem written for music is genuinely a lyric.[1]

Yet it is easy to think even of Romantic works we intuitively
feel to be "lyrical" that violate some or all of these criteria: lyrics
that are long rather than "fairly short," such as *Tintern Abbey;*
lyrics that are wittily rational rather than "emotional," such as

"The Canonization"; lyrics that are impersonal rather than "subjective," such as "Sweeney Among the Nightingales" or "To Autumn"; lyrics that are narrative or dramatic, such as "La Belle
Dame Sans Merci" or "Adam's Curse." Furthermore, efforts to
distinguish subspecies of the lyric have usually been casual and
unsystematic. We speak of "sonnets," "metaphysical lyrics," "love
lyrics," "Elizabethan lyrics," and so on, subdividing according to
form, verse technique, subject, historical period. There is nothing wrong with such classification; I assume that genres are not
fixed Platonic forms, but rather that they acknowledge any perceived category of likeness which may be useful to the critic.
Such haphazard categories, however, do not facilitate a system-
atic mapping of the lyric terrain, which is now vast and various.
    Though Aristotle said little about the lyric other than to dis-
tinguish it as a "manner of imitation," one subordinate insight
in the *Poetics* seems particularly useful in sketching such a map.
Genres are not static: "Tragedy arose, as did comedy, from improvisation," says Aristotle. "Thence tragedy developed little by
little as its possibilities were gradually brought to light, and only
after a long succession of changes did it reach the end of its
development by finding its natural form."[2] I do not want to adopt
Aristotle's implicitly organic and teleological view of literary development; but the history of the lyric, like that of tragedy, shows
that genres change through time. I prefer to compare this process to geographical exploration, to imagine each mode—drama,
narrative, lyric—as a partly uncharted area with unknown
boundaries which the poet explores as he moves (impelled either
by intuitive "improvisation" or conscious experimentation) from
the populated areas into the wilderness. My purpose here is to
speculate about the principles which appear to delimit the lyric
and to propose a tentative map of that territory.

Our century's relative lack of interest in the theory of the lyric—
at least in comparison to other critical problems—is hallowed by
tradition. The enigmatic myth of Orpheus is the ancient world's
most extended commentary on this mode. Plato grudgingly allows hymns and encomia—the praise of gods and heroes—into
his republic.[3] Aristotle's reticence has already been noted, and
the silence remained almost unbroken for centuries. Norman
Maclean remarks that "All the criticism specifically about the

nature of lyric poetry that was written between the Renaissance
and the time of Coleridge, if gathered together, would make not
more than a volume of print."[4] But as the lyric came to supremacy during the eighteenth century, there arose also a theory of
art that both discouraged interest in genre questions and blurred
the distinctions between the lyric and other poetic kinds. The
principal remaining "genre" question in Romantic criticism was
not "What is a lyric?" but "What is poetry?"

The assumption that all poetry, or all true poetry, is in fact
lyric was justified, anticipated, and caused in part by the con-
temporaneous development of expressive theories of art. M. H.
Abrams suggests in *The Mirror and the Lamp* that the changes in
theory and practice were intimately related.[5] But as Paul Hernadi
has shown, critics since the Romantics have constructed theories
based on all four of Abrams's categories of criticism—literature
as mimesis, as rhetoric, as object, or as expression—and some
which elude Abrams's schema entirely.[6] Such theories have of
course implicitly or explicitly included appropriate theories of
the lyric, though the assumption that the lyric is somehow more
"expressive" than the other modes has nevertheless persisted. It
is not encouraging to note that René Wellek concludes, in response to two such genre systems, that "one must abandon attempts to define the general nature of the lyric or the lyrical.
Nothing beyond generalities of the tritest kind can result from
it."[7]

Possibly, however, this remark springs from a frustration with
the limitations of the dominant expressive premise. Wellek's conclusion was elicited by Käte Hamburger's *The Logic of Literature,*
which explores the outer reaches of the premise. Though Hamburger is essentially Aristotelian and mimetic in her assumptions
about drama and fiction, she adopts Hegel's concept of the *Er-
lebnislyrik*,[8] the poem as experience, and refines it in the context
of her linguistic analysis of the lyric mode. Language, she assumes, "has the potential to be either the statement of a subject
about an object, or the function which (in the hands of the
narrator or the dramatist) creatives fictive subjects."[9] Fiction and
drama perform the second of these, and "impart the experience
of non-reality, while the lyric imparts that of reality. . . . We experience it [the lyric] as the statement of a statement subject. *The
much-disputed lyric 'I' is a statement subject.*"[10]

Hamburger's view of the lyric is broadened by her admission (influenced by Husserl) that *Erlebnis,* or experience, is "a comprehensive concept for all acts of consciousness."[11] This definition of experience is an interesting extension of the terms "emotion and imagination" ordinarily used to define the lyric, but it is doubtful that the lyric mode can be distinguished from the others because we experience it as "real" rather than "fictional." Moreover, one wonders how we read lyric poems (such as "To Autumn" or Shakespeare's Sonnet 79) which *have* no "lyric 'I,'" or even poems having an obviously fictional "lyric I," such as Tennyson's "Tithonus" or "Ulysses." Presumably one might expend much effort in seeking connections between authorial expression and the fictional "I" but no adequate definition can simply take an unproblematic "I" for granted.

I assume that lyric poetry, like all other literature, is an artifact, something made by a poet which perhaps represents, but does not "express," experience. However, the theoretical perspective most obviously congruent with this belief, the mimetic, has proved equally unsatisfactory in dealing with the lyric. In America, prior to the past decade or so, the Chicago critics were the most consistently interested in the study of genre,[12] and among them Elder Olson has been the most directly concerned with theory of the lyric (as opposed to the history of such theory, as in the work of Norman Maclean). Olson's discussion is provocative. "A lyric," he writes, "renders the events and activities of the mind" and "presents private thoughts and feelings unknown unless expressed." External events in the lyric mode "are here simply the circumstances of the internal or private events."[13]

These statements are unexceptionable. But further qualifications more clearly reveal that for Olson the drama constitutes the paradigm upon which to construct a parallel "poetics" of the other literary kinds. While Olson does not insist that lyrics have "plot" in the dramatic sense of external action,[14] their tendency to deemphasize external action convinces him that the lyric is inherently a small and "simple" form:

> The lyric consists of a single utterance, usually brief. Epic and tragedy usually involve many characters, in manifold interaction in many incidents, uttering many speeches. . . . It seems that

it might be possible, thus, to arrange the structures of poetry beginning with the very simplest,
in order of increasing complexity, and to see
whether we can locate the lyric among them.[15]

As I suggested earlier, it seems dubious to assume that the
lyric is by definition "small," given the contrary evidence of the
"greater Romantic lyric." An insistence that it _must_ be so seems
to reflect, even in the Aristotelian Olson, the lingering influence
of Poe's dictum that there can be no such thing as a long poem
(for which read "lyric"). But Olson notwithstanding, the lyric can
contain "incidents," "interactions," "many characters"; some few
rare ones contain a complete action or plot.[16] It is also evident
that what we call the lyric exists in many styles and structures.
It might seem perverse to declare that _The Prelude_ and _The Waste
Land_ are both essentially lyrics of enormous complexity, but such
a declaration entails a critical insight worth pursuing.

Olson's implicit use of the drama as the paradigmatic mode
has subtle and dangerous implications for a critic of the lyric.
In another discussion Olson explicitly compares the lyric to a
single speech from a play.[17] And he implies, I think, an assumed
analogy to the drama when he attributes to the lyric "thoughts
and feelings, _unknown unless expressed_" (my emphasis). The familiar question, "Who is speaking, and what is his situation?" is
a favorite gambit for introducing a class to the "close reading"
of a lyric. It can be a valid and fruitful question, and in a peda-
gogical context an almost unavoidable one. Furthermore, the
analogy with the actor's discourse on a stage is perfectly apt for
those lyrics that simulate actual audible speech; for, let us say,
"Dover Beach," "My Last Duchess," or "The Flea."

But for many other poems the analogy cannot hold. Some
lyrics portray silent prayer, meditation, reverie—modes of language which we recognize as _unspoken_, even though the historically earlier examples tend to be structured upon the model of
oral speech. The series of "Directive," "Frost at Midnight,"
and "The Love Song of J. Alfred Prufrock" moves increasingly
toward representation of the associative, nonrational, even the
unconscious, dreaming processes of the mind. And some—certain symbolist poems, perhaps Thomas's "Altar-wise by Owl-
light"—seem primarily to be systems of imagery implying a con-

sciousness which is not articulating or discoursing or expressing itself in the usual sense of the word. Though such lyrics unavoidably use language to represent internal experience, it is a language almost entirely divorced from the functions of speech. Finally, lyrics may portray aspects of experience to which the analogy of the drama is wholly inadequate. Some poems offer glimpses into realities not subject, by definition, to articulation by the consciousness which experiences them: Tennyson's "Mariana," by means of its peculiar third-person perspective, conveys in part dimensions of Mariana's mind far beyond conscious awareness—the Freudian unconscious, the preconscious, or a realm Michael Polyani has discussed as the "tacit."[18] In short, language may represent many processes besides speech. And since lyrics sometimes reveal these shadowy zones of consciousness, we should be wary of any definition of lyric which is bound to the dramatic model of the soliloquy.

Of course, a lyric consists of words.[19] But ideally we should free ourselves from the assumption that these words are *spoken* and regard them, among other possibilities (such as the structuralists' *écriture*), as the poet's "means of imitation," just as stone is the sculptor's. This notion of language as medium is clearer in the work of another mimetic critic, Suzanne Langer. *In Feeling and Form,* she emphasized that the poem is a representation not of speech but of human experience, and is created by the use of the symbol-system we call language: "the poet's business is to create the appearance of 'experiences,' the semblance of events lived and felt, and to organize them so that they constitute a purely and completely experienced reality, a piece of virtual life."[20]

As we have seen, expressive and mimetic theories of the lyric tend to have equal but opposite inadequacies. If pursued rigorously, expressive theories lead one to consider lyric poems merely as quasi-confessional documents, a dimension which may be interesting for certain purposes but which necessarily deflects us from definitive poetic elements. Mimetic theories, however, at least the scrupulously Aristotelian ones, tend to constrict the lyric within too narrow limits, since their ruling analogy with the drama implies a paradigm of the lyric as audible speech.

And yet, the expressive critics seem right about one thing at least: the lyric is definitively concerned with all dimensions of private experience. The mimetic position, on the other hand, seems discerning about another, contradictory, perception: the lyric poem, like most forms of art, *is* a representation; it consists of words so arranged as to create a simulacrum of human experience, not the experience itself. The lyric mode, in fact, is balanced on a paradox: it is a representation of an act of self-expression.

This equivocal and peculiar position accounts, in part, both for the tendency of expressive assumptions to have dominated lyric criticism and for the ultimate inadequacy of these assumptions. One traditional test of a particular lyric's success is the degree to which it is compelling, "real," and true to some level of human experience. Yet the case of the lyric poem is confused and complicated by the nature of the poet's medium—words. Given the inherent meaninglessness of colors or of musical tones, the still life or the sonata is inherently less likely to be taken as a direct personal statement about private experience (much less a characteristic Mondrian or Boulez's *Marteau sans Maître*). But when the poet does all he can to make a statement about an experience authentic, convincing, and "real," it is easy to forget that he is creating an illusion; and when encouraged by Romantic theorists who tell us that the poem is an expression of the poet himself, we are likely to forget that it is, rather, a *representation* of an expression of himself. Of all literary modes, the lyric is best suited to pretending that "fictive discourse" is "natural discourse"; and during the Romantic period it succeeded so well that the Romantic legacy remains today a compelling force.[21]

To keep in mind that the lyric mode may be seen as a representation of an act of self-expression is one step toward formulating a possible, satisfactory definition. But since "expression" raises much the same problems as "speech," one might hope for a better word. We could substitute Langer's "virtual experience," which is an improvement, but this term is relevant to all poetry, not simply to the lyric. What is it that gives the lyric mode its peculiar authority, its deceptive air of "reality," if we reject the notion that it is (in Hamburger's words) a "reality-statement"?

A brief and discriminating comparison of the lyric with the dramatic mode may help to clarify the problem. The assumption that there are three basic kinds of "manners of imitation" is ancient, and is usually attributed to Aristotle's *Poetics* (though some critics reject both the attribution and the adequacy of the tripartite division).[22] Northrop Frye prefers to call these modes "radicals of presentation," emphasizing the rhetorical dimension each mode implies, the varying relationships between audience, work, and author.[23] A drama is acted upon a stage in front of an audience, a lyric in its purest form involves one person speaking or singing, and the narrative involves a teller and a tale, the audience of these latter two being usually a reader rather than a listener. Frye finds the various relationships between author and audience the most interesting of these ratios:

> In drama, the hypothetical or internal characters of the story confront the audience directly, hence the drama is marked by the concealment of the author from his audience. . . . The concealment of the poet's audience from the poet, is presented in the lyric. . . . In *epos*, where the poet faces his audience, we have a mimesis of direct address.[24]

This analysis is accurate, even though as Frye admits, these relationships are "increasingly theoretical," given the modern dominance of the printed word. But a corollary "rhetorical" aspect may offer us a more fruitful distinction between the various modes, and one which more satisfactorily accounts for the lyric's uncanny ability to assume the pretense of natural discourse. That is the relationship between the audience and the "virtual experience" each mode presents. Each, according to its nature, gives, even enforces on, the audience a particular perspective on that experience. Because we watch a drama (or in reading tend to visualize it as action on a stage), we experience it from the outside; thus it is very easy for the dramatist to present physical action in the literal sense, and plot, as Aristotle says, is the "soul" of tragedy. Since dramatic events do not reveal the minds behind them, the dramatist who wishes to give us an authoritative account of a character's motives or feelings must adopt a convention such as the chorus or the soliloquy, which freezes the action momentarily.

But if the drama is life observed, the lyric is life shared; that is, the lyric may be distinguished from other modes by the unique angle of vision it permits its audience—from the inside rather

than the outside of its characters. The lyric perspective is akin
to the one from which we all experience "reality"; the peculiarity
of the lyric poem is that it allows us to assume the perspective
of another individual consciousness.[25] The obvious way one may
"share" another's experience is to hear what he says about it;
this is the extent of the sharing implicit in the analogy of lyric
as dramatic speech. But the lyric goes beyond this point, I think.
Professor Hamburger is correct in associating the lyric's air of
reality with its characteristic use of the first person. A reader
does, arguably, identify more closely with such a speaker; it is
as if the "I" were an empty space in the world of the text which
the reader irresistibly enters. But when that empathy is established, the speaker's language temporarily becomes our language, his experience ours. Depth psychologists have made us
aware of how revealing a choice of words can be (so-called
"Freudian slips"); people who speak a foreign language fluently
often report that they feel their personalities changing as they
speak that other language, that they adopt different facial
expressions and different gestures. But these are truths that
poets have always known, or intuited (one need only compare
Othello's language with Iago's at the beginning of Shakespeare's
play to appreciate the extent to which verbal idiom *is* identity).
Words, in fact, can exert such power over us that to "view" the
world through someone else's words is to put on, for the moment, another consciousness, another's reality.[26] Perhaps this is
the meaning of the myth of Orpheus, the first lyric poet, who
temporarily reshaped nature by the power of his voice.

Assuming that the lyric represents experience and that the
lyric mode causes one to know that experience from within, we
may reformulate a description of the lyric which avoids unnecessary restrictions: the lyric mode exists in literature when the
author induces the reader to know, from within, the virtual experience of a more or less particularized consciousness. When
this aim constitutes the predominant organizing principle of a
poem, we say that the poem is a lyric. The other possible angles
of vision inherent in the other modes are, in the lyric, subordinate to the lyric perspective. Nothing in this definition pre-
cludes us, theoretically, from applying the term "lyric" to certain
prose works; custom and tradition have generally restricted it to
a species of verse. Nevertheless, the distinction between prose

and verse is, in this context, entirely incidental, and in the last chapter I shall briefly consider how the lyric has since permeated the other modes.

This definition obviously still connotes the familiar Romantic qualities of subjectivity, imagination, and emotion; but it also comprehends the more subtle and unfamiliar possibilities in the psychological dimensions characteristic of more modern lyrics, such as "The Love Song of J. Alfred Prufrock." It embraces the mimetic principle while acknowledging the mode's characteristic subject matter: a single speaker's experience of reality, which can be relatively complete or fragmentary—an entire life or one moment of vision, primarily external ("real") or imagined, foreseen or remembered, conscious or unconscious. But in a lyric we always sense the organizing consciousness as a kind of *logos* within the poem, a centripetal force which subordinates argument, narrative, or even other consciousness to itself.

Assuming that the lyric mode represents the experience of an individual consciousness from within, one may then ask what principle could serve as a means of distinguishing among the major subtypes. Obviously a lyric like the medieval "Sumer is ycumen in" is radically different from another expressing similar feelings—such as Wordsworth's "It is the first mild day of March," and different in ways not wholly attributable to poetic technique; the differences seem as much a matter of sensibility, of what is perceived. One possible procedure for drawing a map of the lyric mode is to observe the ratios between the central organizing consciousness of the poem (usually the "speaker") and other relevant consciousnesses: the author's, and others that might, theoretically, appear within the world of the lyric as listeners, interlocutors, or as objects of observation and description. Since "consciousness" is so ungainly, I shall use "speaker" in the following discussion with the proviso that the speaker's function need not be restricted to audible or even articulate speech.

One of these ratios, and the most crucial, is the relation of the "implied poet" (to adopt, and adapt, a term from Wayne Booth) to the voice appearing in the poem. My premise demands the familiar recognition that the speaker of the poem and the author are not identical, no matter how much the poem attempts to seduce us into such an identification. Nevertheless we do have, as readers of any work, a sense of the consciousness that created it, and that remains present "within" or through it. In *The Rhetoric of Fiction*, Booth calls this shadowy self the "implied author," and writes that our sense of him "includes not only the extractable meanings, but also the moral and emotional content of each bit of action and suffering of all the characters. It includes, in short, the intuitive apprehension of a completed artistic whole";[27] and, I would emphasize, in the lyric it constitutes our sense of the consciousness pervading that whole, not as speaker or subject, but as implied artificer. We may feel that we could psychoanalyze the implied author of a lyric; some are cooperative indeed, such as Coleridge, who helpfully supplies us with some of his dreams. It is easy to forget, however, that this information about the "implied poet" is nevertheless a fictional construct and a dimension that can be manipulated by the author as deliberately as any other—rhyme scheme, meter, imagery, all of which may indeed contribute to our sense of implied poet, and which in the usual concentrated lyric have an especially obvious power.

In the lyric, the title appears to be a favorite resource for such manipulation. Wordsworth, intent on poetry as "the spontaneous overflow of powerful feelings," might leave lyrics untitled, as if to imply the spontaneous reality of the experience (as in the poem about the daffodils); or he might give such detail as to time and place (as in *Tintern Abbey*) that he virtually bludgeons the reader into a willing suspension of disbelief concerning the biographical authenticity of the experience.

The ratios between implied poet, speaker of the poem, and other potential speakers that might impinge upon the world of the lyric[28] may be drawn as shown in figure 1.

The first level of distinction, that between "primitive," "pure," and "displaced" lyrics, describes three possible ratios between "implied poet" and the voice of the poem. A "pure" lyric contains the voice we usually associate with the lyric: a first-person speaker virtually identified with the implied poet. It pretends to reveal a consciousness congruent with the implied poet's own. In lyrics using this ratio, there is nothing of *literary* interest to be gained in exploring the sometimes minuscule distance between the implied poet and the speaker. Wordsworth's "I wandered lonely as a cloud" is a "pure" lyric; the "poet-as-I" reveals his "own" consciousness. And though the biographer may point out that the

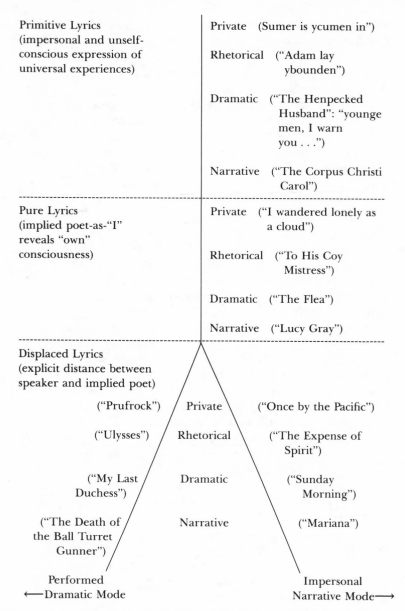

Primitive Lyrics
(impersonal and unself-
conscious expression of
universal experiences)

Private   (Sumer is ycumen in")

Rhetorical   ("Adam lay
            ybounden")

Dramatic   ("The Henpecked
           Husband": "younge
           men, I warn
           you . . .")

Narrative   ("The Corpus Christi
            Carol")

Pure Lyrics
(implied poet-as-"I"
reveals "own"
consciousness)

Private   ("I wandered lonely as
          a cloud")

Rhetorical   ("To His Coy
            Mistress")

Dramatic   ("The Flea")

Narrative   ("Lucy Gray")

Displaced Lyrics
(explicit distance between
speaker and implied poet)

("Prufrock")   Private   ("Once by the Pacific")

("Ulysses")   Rhetorical   ("The Expense of
                          Spirit")

("My Last   Dramatic   ("Sunday
Duchess")   Morning")

("The Death of   Narrative   ("Mariana")
the Ball Turret
Gunner")

Performed   Impersonal
←—Dramatic Mode   Narrative Mode—→

FIGURE 1   A Map of the Lyric Mode

poem is not an accurate representation of Wordsworth's actual experience (we know from Dorothy's journal that she accompanied him on this walk, so the solitude, if not the loneliness, is empirically false), this information adds nothing to our understanding of the poem as a literary artifact, though it may well be of interest to the psychobiographer, or to one exploring the creative process.

If one visualizes the "pure" lyric as the mainstream of the mode, there are a source and two tributaries: the other possible ratios between implied poet and speaker. I call these lyric types "primitive" and "displaced." "Primitive" is the only one of my terms that also tends to correspond to a historical period. By "primitive" I mean "of or pertaining to an earlier stage or state." I might alternately have chosen the term "archetypal," which my dictionary gives as a synonym for primitive, except that I want to avoid the commitment to a particular psychological theory that the word implies. Like primitive paintings—the cave animals of Altamira—the primitive lyric is both intensely expressive of feelingful perceptions (to a degree that may seem magical) and yet completely impersonal and apparently unself-conscious. Leslie Fiedler's adaptation of Jungian concepts to literature, the distinction between "archetype" and "signature," is useful in clarifying my sense of the "primitive" lyric and in defining the differences between a medieval primitive lyric like "O Western Wind" and a modern one like Williams's "The Red Wheelbarrow." An archetype is "any of the immemorial patterns of response to the human situation in its most primitive aspects—death, love, the biological family, the relationship with the Unknown." Signature, however, designates the sum total of individuating factors in a work, the sign of the persona or personality through which an archetype is rendered, and which itself tends to become a subject as well as a means of the poem.[29] As Fiedler notes, *some* congruence of the two is always implicit in a literary work; the work cannot exist unless an individual poet articulates the experience, however universal.

Though medieval lyrics are usually anonymous, anonymity does not insure primitivity, or vice versa. In later periods, experimenters have sometimes returned to primitive techniques (as the Romantics turned to the ballad, imagists to the riddle).[30] For instance, William Carlos Williams's "The Red Wheelbarrow"

invokes the primitive mode. The lyric is impersonal and enigmatic, and exploits the archetypal resonances of "red," "white,"
and "rain." But the mundane particularity of the subject pulls
us back toward "signature": those chickens and that wheelbarrow
are obviously the objects of a private moment of significance and
are perceived in their ordinariness by a particular, individualized
consciousness.

If the primitive lyric tends to deny the presence of an individual maker (hence, perhaps, the nineteenth-century hypothesis of "group" theories of composition for ballads), "displaced"
lyrics emphasize the speaker's separation from the implied poet.
"Displacement" may tend in two different directions: toward the
dramatic or toward the narrative. A "performed" lyric is displaced toward the dramatic mode. Here the speaker transforms
himself into a fictive character, thus opening a potentially ironic
tension within the lyric. The more distinctly this fictive speaker
appears as a character acting and interacting within the world
of the poem, and the more complete the action, the nearer we
move toward drama. The work remains fundamentally a lyric,
however, as long as the poem's "center of gravity" remains in
the lyric purpose, the representation of virtual experience *from
within.* I should emphasize that my typology is a strictly me-
chanical classification of technique. A lyric is "performed" when-
ever we have evidence that the speaker has a different identity—
usually in the sense of a different name—from the implied poet.
Though we may recognize many similarities between Tennyson
and his Ulysses, Eliot and his Prufrock, nevertheless our seeing
through the disguise does not negate the fact that the poet has
ostentatiously assumed it, a fact which must affect our reading
of the poem and need not merely lead us back to what the
performance implies about the author, implied or historical.[31]

In the other principal mode of displacement, the "impersonal"
lyric, the speaker seems to disappear behind the experience,
though our sense of him as a speaking, individualized, perceiving
consciousness may remain quite sharp—as in Keats's "To Autumn." The logical extreme of this line of development is the
omniscient narrator who is everywhere and who knows everything. The sign of the "impersonal" lyric is quite simply the
absence of the self-designating personal pronoun: there is no
"I" or "we." This strategic withdrawal may serve the poet in

various ways. One might risk the generalization that it offers the
lyric poet the illusion of impersonality and universality when he
wishes to escape suspicions of solipsism; or his self-effacement
may permit the sharing of another consciousness, the technique
which critics of fiction sometimes call *erlebte Rede* or "psycho-
narration"[32]—as in Tennyson's "Mariana" or the octave of "Leda
and the Swan."

To summarize, there are three possible ratios between the
speaker, the implied poet, and other possible characters in a lyric
poem: in the "primitive" lyric any sense of implied poet is absent;
he has no particularized identity because the speaker portrays
archetypal experiences in conventional, often formulaic, language. In the "pure" lyric, the speaker is implicitly or explicitly
identified with the implied poet, who is to some extent individualized. In the "displaced" lyric the speaker either assumes a
mask separating him unequivocally from the implied poet ("performed" lyric), or else disappears, leaving the experience portrayed to bear the entire weight of meaning ("impersonal" lyric).

But within these three types one may make further distinctions
relevant to mapping the lyric terrain. Not only may one describe
the relationship of the central organizing consciousness to the
implied poet; one may also observe how the energies of that
consciousness are diffused or concentrated within the poem. I
discern four major possibilities here, which may occur within
any of the other three categories, though some of the possible
types are rare indeed.

The first of these possibilities is the "private," in which the
speaker's energies (whatever his relation to the implied poet) are
essentially turned inward, concerned with himself, with thought,
feeling, memory, perception. The characteristic Romantic lyric
is thus the pure, personal type. The reader is a privileged eaves-
dropper on private experience; it is to this kind of lyric that
Mill's description of the lyric as "utterance overheard" is perfectly apt.[33] The primitive lyric is also frequently private ("Sumer
is ycumen in"); and *performed* private lyrics are not infrequent—
Eliot's "Prufrock" is a good example.

In the second kind, the "rhetorical," the poem is still essentially
self-enclosed, but the speaker's energies are directed outward—
toward an audience, specific or not, real or imagined. But the
poem gives no indication as to how or whether this audience is

being affected by his utterance. "To His Coy Mistress" and "The Canonization" are designed to convince an implied listener of the speaker's argument, but the listener remains completely inscrutable. These are therefore, "pure, rhetorical" lyrics. Pope's *Eloisa to Abelard* is a performed rhetorical lyric; Shakespeare's Sonnet 79, "The expense of spirit," is an impersonal rhetorical lyric.

When, however, the listener *interacts* in some way with the speaker, the lyric becomes a "dramatic" one. The speaker may repeat someone else's words, as in "Adam's Curse," or a listener may make his presence felt in other ways. The envoy in "My Last Duchess" never speaks, as is typical in the dramatic monologue, but the Duke responds to him—his expression of admiration at the Duchess's portrait, his polite gesture in deference to the Duke as they start to descend the stairs. Or in Donne's "The Flea" (pure, dramatic) the lady's skepticism and defiance manifested by her killing of the flea (implicit between stanzas 2 and 3) influences the direction of the argument; without that action, one feels, the poem would not have ended as it does but as a more conventional expression of *carpe diem*.

A fourth and final possibility is the "narrative" lyric. In lyrics of this kind, the speaker tells a story about others. When characters other than the central consciousness appear in the lyric's world, they have the potential of deflecting the lyric mode into the narrative. Within this world, the lyric speaker is placed in the role of storyteller whose business it is to relay a mixture of action and psychological insight which is the narrative's preserve. A favorite Romantic hybrid, the "lyrical ballad," is a lyric because it uses the telling of a story primarily to reveal the consciousness of the teller.

Obviously this definition of the lyric is broader than those that have been traditionally used, and the system of classification I have suggested is unfamiliar. It was evoked by the frustrations encountered in attempting to talk about certain dimensions of the eighteenth-century poems I was reading which seemed to be in the "greater lyric" tradition, but which obviously did not conform to the usual narrower conceptions of the lyric. While this system provides a vocabulary for the following discussion, it might also have broader application. This typology might, for example, offer the possibility of distinguishing between period styles by means other than the thematic or linguistic. It might offer a new means of discussing the criterion of "sincerity" without reference to biography. It might enable one better to articulate the affinities and distinctions among literary modes—fiction, drama, lyric. And it might, at last, enable us to deal more satisfactorily with the rich variety of English lyrics.

2

Epistle into Lyric
Eloisa to Abelard

It is all too easy to visualize the genre critic as Procrustes, butchering texts in the name of categories. Though this reputation may have been deserved by some (such as the eighteenth-century Shakespearean, Nahum Tate), a generic approach need not lead to rigidity or to gross misapprehensions. Procrustes was, after all, rigidly prescriptive, measuring his unhappy guests against a kind of Platonic concept of "ideal visitor." The categories I have suggested are not a priori but a posteriori, not prescriptive but descriptive. But the skeptical reader may rightfully demand evidence that this view of lyric and these terms will enable us to see configurations hitherto unperceived, to make distinctions otherwise missed.

As a test, I want to examine Pope's *Eloisa to Abelard,* a poem which seems to present more difficulties for twentieth-century readers than it did for Pope's contemporaries or, indeed, for the Romantics, among whom it was Pope's most generally admired work. To a large extent, the problems in reading *Eloisa to Abelard* now arise from disputes about the significance of its ending. This final verse paragraph is worth quoting in full:

> May one kind grave unite each hapless name,
> And graft my love immortal on thy fame.
> Then, ages hence, when all my woes are o'er,
> When this rebellious heart shall beat no more;
> If ever chance two wand'ring lovers brings
> To *Paraclete's* white walls, and silver springs,
> O'er the pale marble shall they join their heads,
> And drink the falling tears each other sheds,
> Then sadly say, with mutual pity mov'd,
> Oh may we never love as these have lov'd!
> From the full quire when loud Hosanna's rise,

> And swell the pomp of dreadful sacrifice,
> Amid that scene, if some relenting eye
> Glance on the stone where our cold reliques lie,
> Devotion's self shall steal a thought from heav'n,
> One human tear shall drop, and be forgiv'n.
> And sure if fate some future Bard shall join
> In sad similitude of griefs to mine,
> Condemn'd whole years in absence to deplore,
> And image charms he must behold no more,
> Such if there be, who loves so long, so well;
> Let him our sad, our tender story tell;
> The well-sung woes will soothe my pensive ghost;
> He best can paint 'em who shall feel 'em most.   (343–66)[1]

In his "Argument," Pope praises Eloisa's "celebrated letters" for giving "so lively a picture of the struggles of grace and nature, virtue and passion"; thus some critics, such as Brendan O Hehir, have searched for ways in which "grace" and "virtue" attain supremacy, which, given Pope's Catholicism, they assume to be the only plausible resolution. Langbaum rather casually asserts that Eloisa finally "submits to her religious duty"; Parkin believes that she simply ceases in exhaustion. Krieger finds the poem flawed because Pope has chosen a theme which eludes his "classic need for order." Ackerman finds the conclusion "indeterminate" in itself, though he believes that Eloisa implicitly "accepts her vocation."[2]

At the level of statement, however, Pope's concluding lines are straightforward enough. There are three sentences, three ideas: Eloisa's wish for a somewhat equivocal reunion with Abelard in the grave; her fantasy about the future lovers' visit to this symbol of destructive passion; and finally, the hope that some future poet, who alone can truly know her, will repeat this "sad . . . tender, story." Most puzzling to recent critics is Eloisa's vision of the afterlife, which is as earthly, if not as earthy, as that conceived by Browning's Bishop. Also absent is any sense of divine order; Eloisa speaks of "chance" and "fate" as the presiding deities of this imagined life-in-death.

But however unorthodox in a theological sense, Eloisa's resolution is, in the context of Renaissance love lyrics, highly conventional, echoing in particular Donne's conceit in "The Canonization" and "The Relic" that the saints of love are much like the saints of religion. The miracles vouchsafed by Eloisa's shrine are, however, seen in the evident enlargement of the pilgrims' sensibilities and human sympathy (shown in the "falling tears," and "mutual pity"), and the only eternity she hopes for is that which the "future Bard" may confer, in his monument of "powerful rhyme" (another favorite Renaissance trope).

A sense of release pervades this final paragraph, for it describes movement through time if not through space (the fantasy is controlled by Eloisa's early prediction that "Death, only death, can break the lasting chain / And here, even then, must my cold dust remain" [173–74]). And it also shows her escape, in seeing herself through others' eyes, from the confinements of her own tortured consciousness. Though Eloisa has been fated in life to "image charms [she] may behold no more" she succeeds in "imaging" a final repose for herself. The primary, the sole, movements of the poem are internal rather than external, within the dimensions of emotion and imagination. Therefore *Eloisa to Abelard* belongs to the lyric mode as I have defined it; it enables us to know, from within, the virtual experience of an individual, particularized consciousness. Since Eloisa is obviously distinct from Pope, and a speaker whose energies are directed outwards as she invokes the absent and inscrutable Abelard, it is a lyric of the "performed, rhetorical" type.

But Pope the author of a powerful lyric? Surely this hypothesis violates some traditional assumptions about Pope and about neoclassical poetry. This poem may, however, have grown into a lyric by use of some of the same techniques by which the dramatic monologue (the nineteenth-century lyric kind with which *Eloisa to Abelard* has obvious affinities) later edged away from lyricism, in a desire to escape Romantic confessional subjectivity. It is, perhaps, tempting to see in the closing lines a personal reference, Pope's private pleasure that *he* is the bard who "best can paint" Eloisa's yearnings because he has felt them most. Biographical speculation has been encouraged, too, by Pope's remark to Martha Blount that "the Epistle of Eloise grows warm, and has some breathings of the heart in it, which may make posterity think I was in love."[3] But it is well to notice Pope's playful ambiguity here: is this a coy hint that love is in fact his impulse, or an ironic recognition that the author of love poems need not feel, as a human being, what he expresses? The latter view is an insight into the genesis of lyric poetry on which my assumptions about the lyric are founded.

In any case, biographical speculations are unnecessary here; the poem's generic dimensions can be well established from the text alone. The poem presents a good opportunity to test the workability of my definition of lyric, and to show that a poem's lyricism need have nothing to do with the degree to which it expresses its author's feelings. Instead, the *logos* or primary organizing principle is crucial, and that principle is here the lyrical. Even prior to any close attention to poetic structure, it is clear that Eloisa's letter reveals a firm if confused independence which does not conform to the tenets of her religion, of her lover, or of her poetic creator. To read the poem is to see the world through her eyes, a world in which "heaven," "hell," "grace," "virtue," and even "god" are redefined. Human love is Eloisa's god, and Abelard his earthly incarnation. Her first encounter with him is reminiscent of the Annunciation:

> Thou know'st how guiltless first I met thy flame,
> When love approached me under friendship's name;
> My fancy formed thee of angelic kind. . . .   (59–61)

This seeming Angel, whom Eloisa "loves [as] a man," leads her down "paths of pleasing sense," through an earthly paradise, an Eden:

> . . . happy state! When souls each other draw,
> When love is liberty, and nature, law:
> All then is full, possessing, and possessed
> No craving void left aching in the breast;
> . . . .
> This sure is bliss (if bliss on earth there be)
> And once the lot of Abelard and me.   (91–94; 97–98)

Eloisa's proud refusal of marriage lest she "profane the fires" of *her* "jealous god" strengthens our sense of her independence: "Not Caesar's Empress would I deign to prove; / No, make me mistress to the man I love; / If there be yet another name more free, / More found than mistress, make me that to thee!" (87–90).

It has been generally acknowledged that Eloisa confuses Abelard with God.[4] Less obvious, but equally significant, are the signs that he was also the ambiguously Satanic instrument of her fall. Long after, his "tempting" looks are still alive in her memory (295) and his "fair frame" she admits, was "the cause of all my grief and all my joy" (338). A "guiltless" maiden approached by one believed to be of "angelic kind" may remind the reader of Eve as well as of Mary; certainly Eloisa's subsequent loss was as painful as Eve's. Her "bliss on earth" is lost when the lovers are separated—and Abelard's castration is as irrevocable a sign as earth's wound at the fall of man. "That well-known name awakens all my woe" (30), writes Eloisa as she begins her letter years afterwards, echoing *Paradise Lost* and its history of brief human bliss on earth.

Ostensibly now a bride of Christ, Eloisa remains faithful to the god of her private devotion. She became a nun at the bidding of Abelard: "Sad proof how well a lover can obey!" (172), and she outwardly conforms, though she is inwardly wretched. She has tried "the force of others' prayers" to no avail: "I ought to grieve, but cannot what I ought; / I mourn the lover, not lament the fault!" (183–84). Conscience offers the solutions of religious orthodoxy to soothe the agonies of the heart, which for Eloisa is like trying to cure a burn by thinking about snow. Her sufferings are the result of inflamed consciousness, not conscience. The prospect of forgetting Abelard and her love for him terrifies her ("if I lose my love I lose my all"—118), and she desperately rejects the solution (true religious devotion) which leaves no room for her illicit passion:

> Unequal task! a passion to resign,
> For hearts so touched, so pierced, so lost as mine.
> Ere such a soul regains its peaceful state,
> How often must it love, how often hate!
> How often hope, despair, resent, regret,
> Conceal, disdain,—do all things but forget.   (195–200)

Throughout her letter Eloisa is torn by the alternate claims of her public and private devotions, divine and human love, duty and inclination, oblivion and memory. In redefining all terms of reality (Abelard is God and also Satan, etc.), Eloisa has further restricted her already narrow possibilities for action; she is confined spiritually as well as physically. She will not renounce Abelard, but her love for him prevents comfort in other kinds of

love. The only suspense in *Eloisa to Abelard* (for her as for the
reader) lies in the uncertainty of how she may find *any* peace
within a monastic existence.

Eloisa's consistency even here contributes to our sense of her
strength and individuality; an analysis of its psychological means
shows that Pope has given his heroine a psyche of considerable
complexity. An unconscious or preconscious "logic" (such as later
readers of lyric poems came to expect) controls the transformation of her attitude toward death. From the beginning Eloisa
has known that it is her only means of escape, but only at the
end does she find comfort in this inevitability. She imagines herself as a saint canonized for love, though like the Magdalene
whom she equals in tears, she expects to be an admonition rather
than a pattern. Her "canonization" is reached in much the same
way as Donne's lovers', by sophistical play on the sexual meanings
lurking beneath ordinary language; but the sexual associations
of "die" apparently remain unconscious in Eloisa's mind. Their
presence is pointedly suggested, but only by her late-emerging,
changed attitude toward death.

From first to last, Eloisa conceives of bliss in physical terms.
The blameless Vestal's assumption into heaven is a wedding, with
"Spouse" and "bridal ring": "For her white virgins hymeneals
sings, / To sound of heavenly harps she dies away / And melts
in visions of eternal day" (220–22). And she foresees Abelard's
welcome into paradise in even more explicitly erotic terms: "As
saints embrace you with a love like mine" (342). The language
of mysticism has traditionally used sexual metaphors to express
ineffable spiritual bliss; but in imagining her own situation, Eloisa
reverses the tenor and vehicle of this metaphorical strategy. Since
human, earthly love is her only reality, the conclusion suggests
that in Eloisa's mind death is now acceptable not so much because
it offers escape from this world—she clearly never imagines herself in heaven—but because the tomb is the one bed she can
share again with Abelard. Death offers a "consummation" of
physical existence.

As much as Eloisa yearns for physical reunion with Abelard,
however, she has also longed to restore their spiritual communion, that "happy state . . . where souls each other draw." She
pleads with him to restore at least that part of the relationship
by means of letters:

> Then share thy pain, allow that sad relief;
> Ah, more than share it, give me all thy grief.
> Heaven first taught letters for some wretch's aid,
> Some banished lover or some captive maid;
> They live, they speak, they breathe what love inspires,
> Warm from the soul, and faithful to its fires.
> . . . .
> Speed the soft intercourse from soul to soul,
> And waft a sign from Indes to the pole.   (49–54; 57–58)

Since Abelard, free from earthly passion, has so unequivocally
chosen heavenly over earthly love, she must look elsewhere, to
lovers and poets. In imagining these future lovers and poets who
will know what she has felt, Eloisa rediscovers, however transformed, the last crucial dimension of her paradise lost, human
sympathy; the ending of *Eloisa to Abelard* is both consistent and
complete, a resolution as well as a conclusion.

This paradise is, ironically, inadequate in an absolute sense:
Eloisa's spirit can apparently be soothed only because their bod-
ies are dead, and she is reunited with Abelard, though he is now
dust. Yet her fantasy also dramatizes what the self-deceiving human heart can do to defend and preserve what is most precious
to itself. Eloisa has faith that she will live on in the hearts of
lovers and of poets. Though she herself forgets at last, she will
not be forgotten. Her love will be "immortal" (344) in poetry.

Given this reading of Eloisa's character, the poem's structure
and purpose are congruent with its perspective, that of the first-
person, performed lyric. But how do we account for this allegiance to the lyric mode, given a more obvious and no doubt
consciously chosen imitation of the heroic epistle? It seems likely
that Pope sat down to write a heroic epistle in imitation of Ovid.
Certainly Eloisa has much in common with those highborn heroines of the ancient world who write to their lovers in moments
of crisis and distress. But the term "heroic epistle" denotes merely
these elements of character and situation—it does not necessarily
imply an organizing principle or structure, or a poetic mode as
I have defined it. Ovid's heroines usually lay down their pens
when their story is told; but as we have seen, Eloisa ceases when
she has become reconciled to her fate, and has found peace.

As W. K. Wimsatt has pointed out, however, the concept of
"imitation," which seems so quaintly outmoded to many twen-

tieth-century sensibilities, provided to the eighteenth-century poet a freedom, paradoxically, to be original and experimental.[5] Wimsatt describes such imitation as a "free-running parallel" to a classical model: and this is what Pope has done in choosing a heroine analogous to, but historically much later than, Ovid's. Moreover, Pope's classical "imitation" is further complicated by his choice of another poetic model from his own lyric tradition, a model which he seems intuitively to have chosen as a suitable frame for his cloistered medieval heroine—Milton's "Il Penseroso."

We have become accustomed to the notion that Pope's is a "poetry of allusion."[6] Reuben Brower in particular alerted us to the ways in which Pope habitually incorporated his predecessors into the rich fabric of his own verse. Brower was principally concerned with classical antecedents, but others such as Brooks and Krieger have begun to explore Pope's debt to Milton, which turns out to be considerable.[7] In diction alone, *Eloisa to Abelard* is one of Pope's most obviously Miltonic works. From the opening strains of "deep solitudes and awful cells / Where heavenly-pensive Contemplation dwells / And ever-musing Melancholy reigns," Pope invokes his most immediate master in the English tradition. Krieger has discussed the relation of Eloisa's dilemma to Raphael's hints about angelic lovemaking in *Paradise Lost;* and though editors have long noted Pope's local allusions to "Il Penseroso," the deeper and more significant parallels between these two poems have never been explored. In *Eloisa to Abelard* Pope's model is "Il Penseroso"—a model at once evoked and subverted.

Evidence of this strategy appears both in the language and the structure of *Eloisa to Abelard*. Pope's diction is pervasively "Miltonic," though his un-Miltonic versification has tended to distract readers from these affinities.[8] Eloisa's "I have not yet forgot myself to stone" echoes Milton's "forget thyself to marble" (42).[9] Eloisa's mood of "Black Melancholy" recalls Milton's goddess Melancholy "all in robe of darkest grain" (33), whose visage is "Ore laid with black, staid Wisdom's hue" (16). Eloisa's descriptions of church and Mass echo the Penseroso's "storied Windows richly dight" (159), "pealing Organ," "Service high and Anthems clear / As may with sweetness through mine ear, / Dissolve me into exstasies, / And bring all Heav'n before mine eyes" (159; 161; 163–66). And the word "pensive" appears twice, a subtle framing device, in the second and penultimate lines of *Eloisa to Abelard.*

There are also more fundamental analogies between the two poems. Each is an invocation from beginning to end, and each paints through a variety of experiences the portrait of a contemplative. The Penseroso invokes the goddess Melancholy, as "pensive Nun, devout and pure" (31), while Eloisa (herself a nun, "steadfast," if not "sober and demure") invokes only Abelard, the lost though not forgotten lover. But Eloisa's frantic pleas resonate in a void, while the Penseroso's almost ritualistic formality suggests that his prayer has been granted: Melancholy is already his patroness. We learn the Penseroso's tastes in nature and art, his dreams, his desires to withdraw even farther from life in the "peaceful hermitage / The Hairy Gown and Mossy Cell" (168–69) and of his life's imagined resolution when "old experience do attain / To something like Prophetic strain" (173–74). Eloisa's dominant emotions are quite the opposite: regret, guilt, frustration, claustrophobia. Her dreams are nightmares of loss and despair, or else ambivalently pleasurable, "curst, dear horrors of all-conscious night." The discontinuity of her narrative, as virtue and passion alternately assert control, heightens one's sense of her distress. Yet she also looks forward at last to a "peaceful hermitage," the tomb, and "well-sung woes to soothe [a] pensive ghost."

While the analogies between *Eloisa* and "Il Penseroso" are extensive and intriguing, even a sketchy comparison reveals one crucial fact: as the language and decor and the metaphors of "Il Penseroso" echo in Pope's poem, they are subtly and disquietingly changed. It is as if Pope had fractured "Il Penseroso" and used the pieces to create a strangely altered mosaic picture on the same theme, the contemplative life. The broad design remains the same, but the outlines are distorted, sometimes grotesquely so; the pains rather than the pleasures of melancholy have become the ruling passions of Pope's poem.

We see, for example, what happens to the Penseroso's calm landscape in the eyes of another, unwillingly immured in "studious Cloister's pale" (156). His "high lonely tow'r" (86), "arched walks of twilight groves" (133), "wide-water'd shore, / Swinging slow with sullen roar" (75–76) are transformed in Eloisa's fevered perceptions, imbued with a horrible morbid energy: "round some mouldering tower pale ivy creeps / And low-browed rocks hang nodding o'er the deeps" (243–44). His "Brook / Where no profaner eye may look / . . . And waters murmuring" are in her eyes infused with feelings of sexual frustration, or exhaustion, or both: "These dying gales that pant upon the trees, / The lakes that quiver to the curling breeze" (159–60). And "pensive Melancholy" "all in robe of darkest grain," becomes in Eloisa's mind a figure for profound depression with its accompanying lassitude, gloom, and sense of isolation:

> o'er the twilight groves and dusky caves,
> Long-sounding aisles and intermingled graves,
> Black Melancholy sits, and round her throws,
> A death-like silence, and a dead repose.   (163–66)

The allusions to "Il Penseroso" provide a foil, an index for measuring Eloisa's divergence from the contemplative ideal and the extent of her unrest, for by the early eighteenth century, Milton's celebrated lyric had established a poetic convention for the portrayal of the contemplative life and character. But aside from this thematic dimension, Pope's adoption of this technique insures that *Eloisa to Abelard* belongs to the lyric mode. In "Il Penseroso" the objects of perception symbolically reveal the speaker's psyche, a technique strongly reminiscent of Milton's own master, Spenser. But Spenser's psychological insights emerge from a composite of narrated action and landscape. Dead trees, a sluggish stream, and hooting owls "objectify" Despair's inner nature (*F.Q.*, I, IX), and as Redcrosse speaks with this gloomy character, his responses illustrate Despair's invasion of the human mind. But in "Il Penseroso" objects and action are described by the meditative man himself, the speaker and central character. His, rather than a narrator's, is the organizing consciousness of the work. In other words, we have moved from the narrative to the lyric mode, while retaining the symbolic technique of psychological revelation.

Though Milton's imagery tends to be iconographic, his diction is less conventional than Spenser's, so that the reader of "Il Penseroso" has some sense of an organizing consciousness not only typical but individual. In *Eloisa* we also see everything from the speaker's point of view, and Pope's distortions of Miltonic conventions reveal the idiosyncrasies of Eloisa's particular mind.

(Some years ago Brendan O Hehir pointed out that the instances of "pathetic fallacy" in the poem serve a similar function.)[10]

Finally, "Il Penseroso" informs the conclusion of the poem. In the opening lines, Eloisa knows herself in a place where "heavenly-pensive Contemplation dwells." But she is not at home, nor at peace, being herself the essence of all that is anticontemplative. She cannot desire to "forget [herself] to Marble," the ideal contemplative posture. She wishes to remain defiantly alive to passion and to pain. "I have not yet forgot myself to stone," she says (24). Throughout the letter, Eloisa equates the contemplative ideal with "stone"—the hard, the unfeeling, the cold and dead. Abelard, presumably content, is "cold . . . unmoved and silent grown" (23); for him, "the fates, severely kind, ordain / A cool suspense from pleasure and from pain; / Thy life a long dead calm of fixed repose" (249–51). The life of the "blameless Vestal" is equally marmoreal: "The world forgetting, by the world forgot" (208); "Desires composed, affections ever even" (213).

In her concluding fantasy, however, Eloisa imagines a time when, ironically, she will be "stone" in a quite literal sense—an effigy on a tomb (though one of "pale marble," which however funereal in its connotations, is the stuff of worthy monuments and memorials). And yet this transformation is comforting because Eloisa no longer assumes that oblivion is an inevitable corollary of the metamorphosis, and Abelard "beloved no more." She imagines, as we have seen, a way in which passion can be preserved and the lost spiritual communion restored.

Thus in *Eloisa to Abelard* Pope directs all his poetic skill to creating a speaker who emerges as a complex character of passionate consistency. He succeeds to a remarkable degree, and gives us precisely what his "Argument" announced: "so lively a picture of the struggles of nature and grace, virtue and passion"—psychological verisimilitude, in short, and a poem that conforms to my definition of lyric.

In *Eloisa* Pope undoubtedly was imitating Ovid, though there were more immediate models: many were written during the Renaissance.[11] The category of "heroic epistle," however, is not particularly useful to a critic puzzled by the complexities of *Eloisa to Abelard*, especially its problematic conclusion, for the analogies of character and situation with the model do not extend to poetic mode. "Heroic epistle" and "lyric" are not mutually exclusive

categories, however. And although the heroic epistle, an ancient
and relatively rare kind, is not usually thought of as a lyric genre
(as is the sonnet, for example), its conventions offer obvious op-
portunities for lyricism—for a poem organized according to the
motions of the letter-writer's consciousness. If Pope's conscious
intent was to write a heroic epistle in the manner of Ovid, still
his poetic strategy, that of using a model from his own lyric mode,
insured that the lyric mode would "appropriate" the usually
narrative genre, the epistle.

My thesis is that such "generic appropriation" is the distinctive
mark of the eighteenth-century greater lyric. But before consid-
ering other works in that tradition, it would be helpful to ask
what characteristics of genre theory in the early eighteenth century made such appropriation a plausible and appealing technique. In chapter 1, I argued that a useful distinction can be
made between "mode," which I equate with the Aristotelian
"manner of imitation" or "radical of presentation," and "genre,"
a narrower, less consistently conceived term which may be used
to designate form, content, theme, characteristic structure, or
any other element common to a group of works. Although "tragedy" is traditionally associated with the dramatic mode, its typical
subjects and emotional rhythms might be (and have been) adapted
to either of the other two: the later novels of Thomas Hardy
may be viewed as an appropriation of the tragic by the narrative;
Wordsworth's *Ruined Cottage* may be read as a kind of "lyric
tragedy." Likewise, the sonnet, which is conventionally a "lyric"
form, may on occasion appear within the others. Romeo and
Juliet's first conversation, "If I profane with my unworthiest
hand," is cast in the form of an English sonnet divided between
the two speakers, thus becoming a "dramatic sonnet." Meredith's
lyric, "Lucifer in Starlight," is very near to pure narrative; only
the conventional associations of the sonnet form lead one to
search for a lyric impulse beneath its impersonal surface. In both
these examples, the idiosyncratic shifting of the lyric toward a
different mode becomes itself a significant dimension of meaning. In Shakespeare it is a playful reminder that his characters
so personify ideal romantic love that their conversation "naturally" falls into sonnets; in Meredith it suggests the frustrating
constriction imposed on Lucifer; the sonnet provides an ironic
medium of containment for his vast hubris.

Such "generic appropriation" presupposes two things: a certain flexibility or fluidity of traditional genres, and the power of
the lyric mode. Given the truisms still widely accepted today, that
in the eighteenth century genres were regarded as fixed and
rigid categories, such appropriation might appear unlikely. Recently, however, some critics have seriously questioned this premise concerning genres. One illuminating study, Rosalie Colie's
The Resources of Kind, argues that even in the Renaissance, at the
supposed height of generic rigidity, these kinds were never regarded (nor did they function) as a straitjacket for the poet.
They were instead, Colie suggests, a poetic resource, and "a
means of accounting for connections between topic and treatment within the literary system." Further—and this is Colie's
chief insight for my purposes—the kinds were also understood
as conventions for "*kinds* of knowledge and experience."[12] The
presence of pastoral conventions might therefore signal to the
reader of a work a certain "fix on reality," a particular angle of
vision which would lead him to expect a certain structure, theme,
or resolution, expectations which the author might accept or
violate according to his own purposes.

Ralph Cohen, in an essay entitled "On the Interrelations of
Eighteenth-Century Literary Forms," has applied Colie's insight
to the earlier prose literature of the eighteenth century, suggesting that the presumed rigidity of genres among the neo-
classicists is also a cliché severely in need of revision.[13] Certainly
even a cursory review of this period suggests that it swarmed
with new generic combinations, with hybrids and mutations. No-
where is such innovation more evident than in the significantly
named "novel," another example of "generic appropriation";
Pamela began as an essay in one genre, a series of model epistles,
which inexorably transformed themselves into the narrative now
often regarded as the first novel.

If this distinction between "mode" and "genre" is granted, as
well as Colie's hypothesis about the "resources of kind," then one
may see the poetic evolution that occurred in the eighteenth
century as a parallel to that occurring in philosophy, a change
that has been called "the Copernican revolution in epistemol-
ogy."[14] Just as philosophers recognized that the human subject
was quite as constitutive of meaning as the external object, so
the poetic center of gravity was shifting toward the lyric mode,

the traditional genres being frequently appropriated to its purposes like planets drawn into new orbits by a new, more powerful
sun.

My working hypothesis in this study is quite simply that signs
of such "generic appropriation" as we have seen in *Eloisa to
Abelard* are evident in major and often nonlyric poems throughout the eighteenth century, that such signs are in fact a definitive
characteristic of this verse, and that these works also mark the
rise of the lyric throughout the century. *Eloisa to Abelard* appears
to be a lyric almost in spite of itself. Some genres, such as the
epistle or the pastoral, have such strong lyrical affinities that they
are appropriated with ease. Others, such as epic and tragedy,
almost defy such absorption. But once they have been subsumed
by the lyric mode, the metaphorical implications of the traditional genres become more important, their formal and structural conventions less so. Subordinated to the lyric mode, generic
conventions become something like a pair of magic spectacles
assumed by the lyric speaker, lenses which filter out some elements of literary reality and enhance others. They become de-
terminants of point of view and tone, in their unfamiliar context
a signal to the reader, more explicit than ever, of how this particular speaker views his subject.

The implicit conflict between an inherited genre theory and
the increasing inevitability of the lyric as the chief poetic mode
was resolved by accommodating various nonlyric genres to the
lyric mode with sometimes successful, sometimes rather uneasy
results. But one prior question remains to be explored. What
forces contributed to the rise of the lyric? How did it become,
for the first time in the history of Western literature, the central
and most powerful poetic mode?

3

The Rise of the Lyric

For this chapter, I have adapted Ian Watt's phrase describing the development of prose fiction, for the rise of the lyric and of the novel are not by accident roughly contemporary: many of the same developments that fostered the novel were also hospitable to the lyric. Both literary forms are symptoms of vast and profound changes that were occurring in Western culture as a whole, including philosophy, religion, science, and psychology—changes that entail, collectively, the birth of a recognizably modern frame of mind. But as a literary mode the lyric was not "novel," however radically it was transformed during the eighteenth century; it was not born, but reborn.

One cannot attempt exhaustively to explain this process, but only more or less adequately to describe it, and even that more modest task will be necessarily selective. The following pages could be variously rewritten so as to emphasize quite different patterns of influence. The ones I have chosen, however, seem important largely because they are part of the conscious experience of most poets and critics from the late Renaissance to the Romantics. My point of departure is the metaphorical leitmotif that recurs again and again, early and late—the habit of thinking about poetry, particularly lyric poetry, in religious terms. It begins with the often-repeated notion that "poetry is fallen," and generally concludes, a century later, with the idea that poetry has been reborn. My strategy has been to look for ways in which the vigorous flowering of the secular lyric can plausibly be related to the somewhat earlier apotheosis of the religious lyric in the seventeenth century. By tracing this continuity I do not mean to discount the importance of other "background" influences, such as the well-known radical changes in science and philosophy, much explored by other scholars. But I attend primarily to the system of metaphors that visibly survived in the poetry itself; however "merely figurative" Wordsworth's use of the term "prophet" may be in light of Milton or the Bible, for example, it was a metaphor patently indispensable for him to define his own role as poet and the function of his special kind of poetry.

Thus in the following pages I have grouped together several topics relevant to the rise of the lyric from this selectively religious-literary point of view. They are arranged in order of increasing particularity. First I discuss some persistent metaphors in late seventeenth-century criticism concerning the state and nature of poetry. Second, I consider the origins of one of these, the commonplace observation that the lyric is the oldest, highest, purest form of poetry. Third, I explore the practice of meditation on the creation and the Book of Job, two established models embodying patterns for organizing experience (small-scale myths, we might call them) which together suggest two complementary responses to an epistemological question any lyric poet implicitly faces: how can individual experience lead one to the wisdom and authority that the voice of a "greater lyric" demands? Next I analyze Milton's poetic illustration of the problem in "Il Penseroso," a work which I see as a paradigm that is continually being refracted, distorted, and creatively rewritten throughout the subsequent century. Last I consider some of the technical problems that the poet of the greater lyric must solve, by suggesting that the "Pindarick," or irregular ode, with its intrinsic or "organic" rather than fixed formal unity, offered a usable pattern for the freedom and flexibility required by a new era of bold poetic experimenters leading (more gradually and slowly than we habitually assume) into the Romantic age.

The Waning of the Renaissance

During the past few decades scholars have become increasingly dissatisfied with the labels usually attached to the early years of the eighteenth century. Shall we call them "The Age of Reason," "neoclassicism," or "Augustan"? Various thoughtful people have found good reasons for rejecting each of these names, just as others had good reasons for proposing them in the first place.[1] But we need to be careful about such terms, as R. S. Crane once pointed out, because they usually become tacit hypotheses subtly controlling our conception of a particular time.[2]

Lawrence Lipking has written that "The historian of an art needs an innocent eye, perceptions that fall outside the usual categories."[3] Anyone tracing the rise of the lyric is certainly forced to ignore the established boundaries, for this process blurs several of the usual lines of demarcation. The rise of the lyric—by which I mean this mode's gradual but thoroughgoing appropriation, in practice, of the larger traditional genres, and the concurrent establishment of an expressive theory of literature— is perceptible as early as the third and fourth decades of the seventeenth century. From my perspective in this book, the years from about 1660 to 1745 must be understood not only as the "Restoration" and "neoclassical" periods but also as the final years of the Renaissance. Certain notions of poetry which had ruled for over two centuries were powerful until virtually the middle of the eighteenth century, and what is now regarded as the most characteristic poetry of these years was occupied with exploring the remaining possibilities of an almost exhausted tra- dition. Yet the new developments were deeply rooted in the old. The rise of the lyric was in many ways an inevitable outgrowth of universal assumptions about poetry, the poet, and the true poetic themes that were partly definitive of the literary Renais- sance—even though the eventual result was to be so different as to suggest that a true revolution had occurred.

This period, 1660–1745, has been called "the Silver Age of the European Renaissance," but there are also reasons for char- acterizing it as "the waning of the Renaissance."[4] While English literature between Milton and Swift is undoubtedly "exuberant" (another term recently favored), its typical preoccupations just as obviously constitute the final phase of the long previous tra- dition.[5] The "neoclassicism" of the early eighteenth century—a sometimes arid obsession with "rules" and other supposedly clas- sical practices—merely fulfills implications of the earlier rebirth of ancient learning. Critics' emphasis on the didactic function of literature, for example, constitutes an insistence on half of Hor- ace's dual principle that literature should instruct and delight. Literary "delight" resided primarily in a virtuoso handling of irony. The predominance of this mode in the period's acknowl- edged masterpieces, such as *The Rape of the Lock*, *The Dunciad*, and *Gulliver's Travels*, also suggests the self-consciousness so char- acteristic of the end of a tradition. Certainly "Augustan" litera-

ture demands considerable literary sophistication of its readers;
it is a literature notoriously difficult to study outside the cultural
context it invokes. And that context tends to be Renaissance
generic conventions. *The Dunciad* becomes perhaps a better poem,
certainly a different and an easier one, for the reader who is
intimate with *The Iliad* and *Paradise Lost*. A good case could be
made for Pope as the last Renaissance poet, an artist whose
destiny was to create (as Debussy said of Wagner) a magnificent
sunset which could only briefly have been mistaken for a sunrise.

Equally striking, and congruent with the literary dominance
of the ironic mode, is the pessimism, cynicism, and revulsion
from the human condition common among the characteristic
voices of the early eighteenth century. (Huizinga notes a similar
mood in the waning years of the Middle Ages;[6] something like
it was conspicuous in the late Romantic *fin de siècle* attitude.)
Donald Greene has argued persuasively that "Augustinianism"
would be more apt than "Augustan" to describe those poets who
were so conscious of man's fallen state, his inherent depravity.
One might quibble that "Augustinianism" is more accurately
qualified as "St. Augustine as read by Calvin" (who read him
very closely indeed), but this qualification merely emphasizes the
nature of the era's limited faith in natural human goodness, at
least among the major poets.[7] In such minds this pessimism
manifests itself in an emerging sense that the poet is oppressed
by the burden of the past. As Walter Jackson Bate suggests, a
sense that modern poets were helpless in the face of so much
past greatness weighed heavily upon them, and was yet another
sign of exhaustion.[8]

But nothing more strongly suggests that this period should be
regarded as the waning of the Renaissance than its literary criticism. Aside from Dryden, there are no really distinguished critics during these years, and he was primarily preoccupied with
drama; even Dennis, who is the most original thinker of the lot,
is remembered chiefly as the object of Pope's vituperation. The
names important to this history tend to be only vaguely familiar:
Norris, Ogilvie, Cleeve, Temple, Gildon, Blackmore, Trapp. Yet
they are remarkably consistent among themselves and all the
more interesting because they do so little to modify the major
critical premises of the Renaissance, articulated, for example, in
Sidney's *Apology* more than a century earlier. Their writings con-

stitute, in fact, the last reiteration of Renaissance critical assumptions and truisms, before they were to be transmuted, almost beyond recognition, into the assumptions and truisms of Romanticism.

Sidney's motives for defending poetry were still felt by his successors—"to make a pittiful defence of poore Poetry, which from almost the highest estimation of learning is fallen to be the laughingstocke of children."[9] At the end of the seventeenth century, the old Platonic argument still flourished that poetry, being fiction, was falsehood and, for some, the lure and snare of the devil. Such an attack, in Stephen Gosson's "School for Abuse," had been Sidney's ostensible occasion for the *Apology,* and similar attitudes are encountered as late as 1712 in Charles Gildon's *Complete Art of Poetry.*[10] Besides a common air of defensiveness, one finds other ideas and arguments from Sidney in the later critics; one might fill a monograph with the echoes, parallels, even wholesale importations of Sidney's words (themselves hardly new) in late seventeenth- and early eighteenth-century English critics.

Many still wrote, for instance, that poetry had seriously declined from a glorious past. In Sir Thomas Pope Blount's *De Re Poetica* (1694), a compendium of opinions "selected out of the best choicest criticks" and arranged by topics, an early section is entitled "*Poetry* Encourag'd in former Ages: but discourag'd in this."[11] The decline and fall of poetry is described and documented in the late seventeenth century with an urgency, a bitterness, foreign to Sidney. According to John Norris, "this most Excellent and Divine Art of *Poetry,* has of late been so cheapened and depreciated . . . that *Poetry* is grown almost out of *Repute,* and men come strongly prejudiced against any thing of this Kind, as expecting nothing but *Froth* and *Emptiness.*"[12] "*Poets* are *now* reckon'd among that *Class* of *Beings* that carry along with them no real Use, or Profit; but serve only to fill up the *Vacuities* of the *Creation,*" writes Charles Cleeve.[13]

Fallen poetry has become in the minds of many a fallen woman, "a common Prostitute to Lust, Flattery, Ignorance and Ambition." Dennis argues that "if Poetry be more philosophical, and more instructive, than History . . . why then that Art . . . with which a great many Writers of Verses and Plays debauch and corrupt the People, is a thing to which Poetry is as directly contrary, as a Virgin to a Whore."[14] Oldham speculates that if "mighty Sappho" should be reborn, and hope to write, "She must to Creswell's trudge to mend her gains, / And lett her *Tail* to hire, as well as *Brains*."[15] And so Dennis begins an effort of restoration, his "Grounds of Criticism in Poetry" (1704), with a premise: "That poetry is miserably fall'n, is, I suppose, granted."[16]

This fall seems tragic in the context of these critics' surviving fantasies of a cultural paradise lost, when poets were honored in their own country at least, and true to their own divine gifts. As Sidney had written, "Among the Romans a Poet was called *Vates*, which is as much as a Diviner, Fore-seer, or Prophet." He continues: "The Greekes called him a Poet, which name hath as the most excellent, gone through other languages. It commeth of this work *Poiein, which is to make*."[17] The argument from etymology is still prominent a century later. Samuel Woodford remarks that "The *Grecians*, to shew the high Veneration they had for their *Poets*, call'd 'em *Makers* or *Creators* . . . and the *Romans* . . . styl'd 'em *Prophets*."[18] Lord Roscommon optimistically declares that "By secret Influence of Indulgent Skies, / *Empire*, and *Poesie* together rise."[19] And others elaborate in detail the honors poetry and the poet once enjoyed. Cleeve reminds his readers that "the Famous *Alcaenus* . . . used to make his Speeches in *Verse* at the head of his Army. . . . The great *Scipio* had *Ennius* always in his Camp. . . . In those Times, there was scarce any Great Man without his *Poeta à Latere*."[20]

The causes of this unfortunate fall are not obscure. Though Cleeve places some blame on the poets themselves for choosing trivial themes, the fall of poetry is on the whole regarded as another aspect of that decay of nature initiated by the loss of Eden. It is "no small Argument to the incredulous of that first accursed fall of *Adam*," writes Sidney, "sith our erected Wit maketh us know what perfection is, and yet our infected Will keepeth us from reaching unto it."[21] Gildon appropriates that statement virtually word for word.[22] And Trapp explains the decline of poetry in one terse sentence: "In the Course of Time, Poetry, which had hitherto depended wholly upon Nature, and knew not the Name of Art, by the Corruption of Mankind grew itself corrupted."[23] Thus the logical corollary of Dennis's belief in the fall of poetry is the one purpose of his criticism: "To restore Poetry to all its Greatness, and to all its Innocence."[24]

Finally, the continuing power of Renaissance assumptions remains in statements about the relation of art to nature and about poetry's power for its audience. The Aristotelian principle of mimesis is universally accepted, early and late. "Poesie therefore is an arte of imitation, for so Aristotle termeth it in his word *Mimesis*," wrote Sidney, "that is to say, a representing, counterfetting, or figuring foorth: to speak metaphorically, a speaking picture."[25] This idea is still the accepted commonplace when Trapp writes (echoing Horace also) that painting and poetry "both agree, in representing to the Mind Images of Things, and ought both of them to be govern'd by Nature and Probability."[26]

The other principle of almost canonical authority is Horace's dictum that the purpose of such imitation is instruction and delight. Sidney had written:

> [Poets] indeede doo meerely make to imitate, and imitate both to delight and teach, and delight to move men to take that goodnes in hande, which without delight they would flye as from a stranger; and teach, to make them know that goodnes whereunto they are mooved, which being the noblest scope to which ever any learning was directed. . . .[27]

Dennis's statement in "The Grounds of Criticism" is not much different: "Poetry then is an Art, by which a Poet excites Passion (and for that Cause entertains Sense) in order to satisfy and improve, to delight and reform the Mind, and so to make Mankind happier and better: from which it appears that Poetry has two Ends, a subordinate, and a final one; the subordinate one is Pleasure, and the final one is Instruction."[28]

At the beginning of the eighteenth century, then, the terms of critical discussions were still set in the patterns established by Aristotle and Horace, as interpreted by Sidney and other Renaissance writers over a century previously. It was generally acknowledged that poetry is an art which represents nature to man for the purpose of instructing and delighting. Like all earthly goodness, however, poetry had fallen through the corruption of man, fallen far from its once high and honorable function. And yet, a hundred years later, Shelley, in another famous defense of poetry, was to write that "the literature of England has arisen

... as it were from a new birth."[29] His older contemporary
Wordsworth declares that, through the agency of the prophetic
poet, paradise might be regained on earth, the "simple produce
of the common day."[30]

Two great changes had occurred in that intervening century,
changes that mark the rise of the lyric: the mimetic theory of
poetry had been largely transformed into an expressive one, and
poetry itself had become virtually identified with the lyric mode.
It is reasonable to speculate that this development is intimately
related to the critics' pessimism at the beginning of the eighteenth century. If poets felt oppressed by the terrible burden of
past epic and tragic poetry, the lyric mode at least was not much
claimed by distinguished precursors: it seemed a *terra incognita*
awaiting its Cortez if not its Columbus. Though critics repeatedly
declared that modern poetry was fallen and degraded, a number
of forces continuous with the late Renaissance had guided them
to the emerging conclusion that lyric poetry was the purest,
holiest, oldest kind, and therefore that best suited to the restoration of their art.

Puritan Poetics and Poetical Puritans

These late seventeenth-century critics, however secular, were Puritans of a sort. They wished to free poetry from its current
degradation. Reading these critics who flourished around the
turn of the eighteenth century, one is struck by their consistency,
not only of theme but of metaphor. When speaking of the purpose and origins of poetry and the role of the poet, they tend
to borrow the vocabulary of theology. The notion that a poet is
somehow sacred may be traced back at least as far as Plato. But
these critics have a Calvinistic slant. They reiterate that poetry
is fallen and (like fallen man) is foul and debased; that it is,
likewise, awaiting restoration.

The theological cast of their discussion does not necessarily
arise from consciously chosen metaphors, however. It is an inherited Renaissance convention. It appears prominently in Sidney's *Apology*, for example, a work Restoration critics obviously
knew, quoted, and copied. In the following discussion I shall use
Sidney's essay as a convenient and familiar source of earlier
Renaissance critical commonplaces, although one should remember that his was by no means the only expression of these

ideas. The *Apology* is usually admired as a synthesis of Renaissance classicism, but Sidney's use of biblical examples as support at crucial points in his argument is more significant as a harbinger of the rise of the lyric. After explaining the etymology of *Vates,* Sidney writes:

> And may not I presume a little further . . . and say that the holy *Davids* Psalmes are a divine Poem? If I doo, I shall not do it without the testimonie of great learned men, both ancient and moderne: but even the name Psalmes will speake for mee, which, being interpreted, is nothing but songes.[31]

Explicating the concept of "imitation," Sidney again refers to the Bible. "The chiefe both in antiquitie and excellencie were they that did imitate the inconceivable excellencies of GOD. Such were *David* in his Psalmes, *Salomon* in his song of Songs, in his Ecclesiastes, and Prouerbs, *Moses* and *Debora* in theyr Hymnes, and the writer of *Iob.*"[32] And countering the argument that poetry is composed of falsehoods, Sidney observes that Christ himself used fictions, stories "which by the learned Divines are thought not historicall acts, but instructing Parables," a technique admirably effective in its didactic power, as he himself testifies: "Truly, for my selfe, mee seems I see before my eyes the lost Childes disdainfull prodigality, turned to envie a Swines dinner."[33]

Sidney's ideas here are as conventional as his use of classical sources, for the *Apology* is typical of Renaissance art in its reconciliation of Christian with classical, ancient with modern. It also shows that the conclusions derived by Protestant scholars in their reexamination of the Bible as a literary text were being rapidly assimilated into secular literary theory, a line of influence which would remain active into the nineteenth century: witness Wordsworth's allusion in the *Preface of 1815* to certain portions of the Scriptures as the highest lyric poetry, and Coleridge's *Statesman's Manual* which continues the traditional interest in the Bible as a literary text. We have already noted a Calvinist perspective in the Renaissance conception of poetry as something good corrupted, with mankind, into a state of woeful depravity. Shelley's words about the "rebirth" of English letters, quoted above, reveal the continuity of that metaphorical habit, and they are M. H. Abrams's point of departure in *Natural Supernaturalism,* which explores the prevalent secular use of theological metaphors among the Romantics to describe the nature and function of poetry. It seems that in Sidney, and even more in Gildon, Trapp, Blackmore, Dennis, and the other late Renaissance critics who speak of the ideal poet as a prophet and of poetry as a means of moving men toward the good, we observe the birth of this metaphor within the English tradition.

The definitive explication of the source of such attitudes is found in Barbara K. Lewalski's *Protestant Poetics and the Seventeenth-Century Religious Lyric,* which argues that the Protestant emphasis on the Bible as God's book, a book "requiring philological and literary analysis," had a powerful effect on Protestant poetics, and made the Bible "normative for poetic art as well as for spiritual truth." The consequent attitudes about genre, symbolic modes, and the decorum of poetic language and themes exerted a powerful stimulus on the religious poets of the seventeenth century, such as Donne, Herbert, Vaughan, Traherne, and the American Edward Taylor.[34]

Lewalski is concerned with the influence of such "Protestant poetics" on the religious lyric, precisely where one might expect to find it. But the assumptions of "Protestant poetics" were also evident during the same period in secular poetry and criticism; most important in this context, they had a far-reaching influence on the establishment of the lyric as the central poetic mode. (It is true, of course, that in the seventeenth century the making of a clear distinction between "religious" and "secular" was not habitual.) An important element in this influence was the prominent attention to the lyrical genus in the Bible. Lewalski emphasizes that the Psalms were especially valued as poetic models because they were believed to mirror the entire range of human spiritual experience. In Calvin's words,

> Not without cause am I wont to terme this book
> [the Psalms] the Anatomy of all the partes of the
> Soule, inasmuch as a man shal not find any af-
> fection in himselfe, wherof the Image appeereth
> not in this glasse. Yea rather, the holy Ghost hath
> heere lyvely set out before our eyes, all the
> greefes, sorowes, feares, doutes, hopes, cares,
> anguishes, and finally all trublesome motions

wherewith mennes mindes are woont to be
turmoyled.[35]

Such psychological themes are the definitive matter of lyric poetry. But establishing the Psalms, believed to be lyrics, as the
model did more than merely encourage the poet to look in his
heart and write.

Those critics of the later seventeenth century who wished to
purify poetry, to return it to its high and holy origins, could find
support from the theologians, who had elaborated and amplified
the classical idea (never of much interest among ambitious poets)
that the highest, purest, oldest form of poetry is the lyrical en-
comium, the poetry of praise. This opinion, by 1700, had become
a cliché in all quarters. Dryden remarks that "the first *Specimen*
of [poetry] was certainly shewn in the Praises of the Deity, and
Prayers to him; And as they are of *Natural Obligation,* so they
are likewise of *Divine Institution.*"[36] According to Temple, "It appears that Poetry was the first sort of Writing . . . the Psalms of
David would be the first Writings we find in Hebrew; and next
to them, the Song of *Solomon,* which was written when he was
young, and *Ecclesiastes* when he was old."[37] Says Gildon, "The
first Poetry was certainly the Praise of God and Thanksgiving
of Man for the natural Benefits bestowed on him by Heaven;
and this was sung for the greater Solemnity to Music."[38] Trapp
concurs: "It is certain in the earlier Ages of the World it was
usual to sing hymns to the Honor of God."[39]

The growing authority of the lyric also has much effect upon
discussion of various critical questions: standards of judgment,
the concept of imitation, effects on the audience, the role of the
poet. Trapp, for example, finds the lyric's inherent superiority
grounded in its intimate relation to human psychology and hence
to verisimilitude: "if we consider the internal Motions of the
Soule, it will seem very probable that Poetry, which is so peculiarly adapted to express the several Emotions of Joy, or Praise,
or Gratitude, owes its Rise to Nature herself." He concludes a
series of general remarks on the lyric with a statement about its
preeminence that was perhaps surprising in 1714: "The lyric
poem . . . is, of all kinds of Poetry, the most poetical; and is as
distinct, both in Style and Thought, from the rest, as Poetry is
in general from Prose."[40]

To "consider the internal motions of the soul" as a telling, perhaps as the primary, critical criterion, as Trapp does, would once have been unthinkable. Admittedly, lyric poets had in practice implicitly conformed to this standard, but it had not been a traditional caveat. An earlier case related to Trapp's remark is Longinus's "On the Sublime." A similar principle pervades that document, but it was largely ignored in England until the second decade of the eighteenth century; and its sudden popularity then is plausibly attributable to the fact that it provided classical authority for then-established taste.[41]

Aside from emphasis on the lyrical portions of the Bible as the authoritative model, Protestants emphasized other notions and practices which also had wide effects. One such idea was belief in introspection as a means to truth. Consequent interest in psychology—a study fully conceived but still an embryonic science—was by 1700 beginning to have an effect on the mimetic premise that had served as a foundation of criticism since classical antiquity. Critics still asserted that poetry is an imitation, but they were now invariably quick to note that it imitates more than external action. Granville, Lord Lansdowne, begins his verse essay, "Upon Unnatural Flights in Poetry," with the statement that "Poets are Limmers of another kind, / To copy out Ideas in the Mind; / Words are the paint by which their thoughts are shown, / And Nature is their Object to be drawn."[42] Trapp modifies Vossius's strict interpretation of Aristotle in his own definition of poetry:

> [Aristotle] thought therefore that not only Actions but manners, and Affections, were capable of being imitated. . . . Both [painters and poets] give us Draughts of the Body, as well as the Soul; but with this difference, that the former is chiefly expressed by Painting, the latter by Poetry.[43]

Dryden remarks that "to describe the *Passions* naturally, and to move them artfully, is one of the greatest Commendations that can be given to a *Poet*."[44] (Here a rhetorical and a quasi-expressive criterion come to the fore.)

This emphasis on the psychological "objects" of poetic imitation (in antiquity usually attributed mainly to music) also affected the ways in which critics were beginning to describe poetry's rhetorical dimension as well. The belief—or fear—that poetry engages the passions of its readers is often present in criticism from Plato onwards, and it was this engagement that evoked the distrust of the more radical Puritans, who believed poetry to be playing with hellfire. Sidney had, however, argued that poetry shows the reader a moving image of perfection, otherwise unavailable in this world. (And in his invocation of biblical examples he implicitly put the lyric above all others.) By the late seventeenth century, critics were speculating in greater detail about the mechanics of reader response: *how* the passions might be aroused and moved toward the good. An unexpected insight into this question and the persisting theological roots of its orthodox answer appears in a little-known work by Richard Baxter, the great Protestant divine.

In 1681 Baxter published a volume of lyrics called *Poetical Fragments*, to which he appended a scriptural epigraph: "Speaking to your selves in Psalms and Hymns, and Spiritual Songs, singing and making Melody in your hearts to the Lord" (Eph. 5:19). In the preface, Baxter defends the value both of human passion and of the poetry which may serve to communicate it:

> I confess when God awakeneth in me those passions which I account rational and holy, I am so far from condeming them, that I think I was half a Fool before, and have small comfort in sleepy Reason. Lay by all the passionate part of Love and Joy, and it will be hard to have any pleasant thoughts of Heaven.[45]

Here is Sidney's argument echoed again—the value of a literary experience of the good—but now it is more explicitly concerned with psychological experience, so that it also looks forward to the expressive theories of the later eighteenth century, not to didactic purposes only. Baxter continues: "But as [these poems] were mostly written in various Passions, so passion hath now thrust them out into the World, God having taken away the Dear Companion of the last Nineteen Years of my life."[46]

Baxter's secular contemporaries are equally concerned with the power of poetry to express and to engage human passion. Sir Richard Blackmore writes, "Tis in the power of Poetry to insinuate into the inmost Recesses of the Mind, to touch any

Spring that moves the Heart, to agitate the Soul with a sort of Affection, and transform it into any Shape or Posture it thinks fit."[47] Or Gildon: "I think it may easily be made out, that there is nothing has a greater Power or Influence on the Heart than Poetry. . . . There is indeed no manner of Question but that true Poetry has Force to raise the Passions, and to allay them, to change and to extinguish them."[48] And poetry's engagement of passions was to be one of the fundamentals of Dennis's poetics.

The poet's power to "transform [the mind] into any Shape or Posture it thinks fit" is an awesome responsibility, though one perfectly congruent with the ancient tradition of poet as *Vates,* and one to which the lyric seemed well adapted. But recognition of this power was not enough. If some late seventeenth-century poets believed that the lyric was the oldest, purest, holiest kind of poetry, there were still relatively few predecessors, models, or examples in English. Furthermore, although their language was rich in the smaller lyric kinds such as songs and sonnets, there were of the "greater lyrics" a mere handful of odes. Thus arose a need to find the proper themes, voices, and poetic forms to inspire a new lyrical impulse. The world was all before them— and as it happened, the world of nature, in particular, became more and more frequently their theme, or at least the indispensable context of the human life they sought to explore.

Two Methods of "Propheting" from Experience

Seventeenth-century Protestant poets such as Herbert and Vaughan wrote lyrics in order to tell the intimate history of their own colloquies with God, sequences like the Psalms' "Anatomy of the Soule," as Calvin called it. Such poems had two qualities which, once established as conventions, lyric poets could seemingly no longer avoid: the lyric had been used as a vehicle for a subject of the highest seriousness, religion; and in conjunction with that subject, a lyric voice of the minutest psychological verisimilitude had now become familiar. In these poems, the reader feels the unique person in the poem as never before in religious verse. The religious lyric had thus moved, in my terms, from the primitive (as in the medieval "Adam lay y-bounden") to what I have called the pure lyric type (see chapter 1).

But not all poets were so orthodox, nor did lyrical poets wish to restrict themselves to religious subjects (though a remarkable number of the now-forgotten poems are biblical paraphrases and imitations). Furthermore, it may be that there was simply no important perceived difference between writing poems about God or poems about nature, the latter having a more intensely sacramental significance than they would even a century later in Wordsworth, for this was the climactic era of physico-theology, when Bishop Bentley consulted Newton regarding a sermon arguing that the law of gravity was evidence of divine providence.

To such poets, theology and literary tradition offered two models with biblical and doctrinal authority whose influence can be seen in the organization and themes of greater lyrics throughout the subsequent century, long after explicit allusions to the models have disappeared. Both pointed to ways in which the private self bound by limited knowledge might be transformed into a prophet, the traditional proper voice of the greater lyric. These were the Protestant practice of meditation on the creatures and on the Book of Job. These reveal two complementary modes of apprehending and responding to God, in both cases to God as he is manifested through nature—a fact of obvious significance for the future history of poetry.

Meditation on the Creatures

It would be difficult, perhaps impossible, to separate the combined complex literary influences of Protestantism, empiricism, and late seventeenth-century scientific experimentation. Clergymen devoted themselves to physico-theology; the physicist Sir Robert Boyle confessed to a conversion in a thunderstorm; Newton is reputed to have valued his commentary on the Book of Daniel more than the *Principia*. In the Calvinist tradition most emphatically, interest in nature—already spurred by science—was validated by biblical assurance that "the heavens declare the glory of God, the firmament sheweth his handiwork" (Psalm 19:1). This enthusiasm also made nature an inevitable subject for the lyric poet attempting to reassume his vatic role, and the practice of "meditation on the creatures" as encouraged by seventeenth-century Protestantism, offered one means of organizing literary responses to the natural order.

It is generally accepted that Calvin dominated English Protestant theology until the mid-seventeenth century.[49] His voluminous biblical commentaries as well as the *Institutes* reveal one main source of the changing attitudes toward nature. "Nearly all the wisdom we possess . . . consists of two parts," wrote Calvin, "the knowledge of God and of ourselves."[50] Protestant belief concerning the "Book of the Creatures" was grounded on the premise that a knowledge of the self and the rest of creation is one path to the knowledge of God. Calvin taught that man's responses to nature were a primary and authentic means to both: the reading of nature was as much a sacred duty as the study of God's other text, the Bible.

According to St. Paul, "The natural man receiveth not the things of the spirit, of God . . . because they are spiritually discerned" (1 Cor. 2:14). Original sin had, in Calvin's words, left those mental faculties which are the image of God in man "defaced, mutilated, and disease-ridden."[51] (One recalls Sidney's allusion to "our infected will.") But election and justification initiate a process of restoration, a process which continues throughout life. Thus imputed grace is, from the sinner's point of view, a pair of spectacles enabling myopic, astigmatic "natural man" to see (however dimly) divine will and wisdom in God's two books. Thus justified, the Christian should cultivate his powers of "spiritual discernment" so that he might "enjoy a Paradise of heavenly delights on earth."[52]

Nature, Calvin argues, affords man aesthetic experience of the divine attributes—love and wrath, wisdom and power—but no evidence concerning points of doctrine. So rather than distrusting and discounting empirical experience, as the patristic writers had tended to do,[53] Calvin and his followers argued that God compels us to make use of the senses (in spite of their dangerous propensities to sensuality and skepticism). Nature, Calvin says, is "generall to all men," and here man may experience power infinitely greater than himself. "If a man consider all the effects of a tempest, they [sic] see things that could not bee believed if they were not known by experience," he writes.[54] Richard Baxter elaborates on this point:

> the meer pure work of Faith, hath many disadvantages with us, in comparison with the work of Sense. Faith is imperfect, for we are renewed but in part; but Sense hath its strength, according to the strength of the flesh. . . . Faith is super-

> natural, and therefore prone to declining, and
> to languish . . . but sense is natural, and there-
> fore continueth while nature continueth. The
> object of Faith is far off . . . but the object of
> Sense is close at hand.
>
> It is no easie matter to rejoyce at that which
> we never saw, nor never knew the man that did
> see it . . . but to rejoyce in that which we see and
> feel, in that which we have hold of, and posses-
> sion already; that is not difficult.[55]

In nature's violence, man might experience some intimation of
divine wrath; in its beauty and order, divine wisdom and mercy.
Fear, in particular, might well be God's hammer to mollify man's
hard heart, preparatory to the imputing of grace.

But nature's usefulness did not end with the chastened sinner's
conversion. Instead, the creation revealed to the incipient saint
shades of meaning heretofore unperceived. Admiration of the
creation was one means of obeying St. Paul's injunction to make
the sacrifice of praise. As Joseph Hall cautions, "The creatures
are halfe lost if wee only employ them, not learne something of
them; GOD is wronged if his creatures be unregarded."[56] And
careful observation of nature might teach man useful lessons,
both moral and natural: "As an Interpreter in a strange Country
is necessary for a traveller that is ignorant of Languages (or else
he should perish,) so is knowledge and learning unto us poor
Pilgrims in this our Perigrination, out of Paradice, unto Paradice,"
wrote Edward Topsell in his preface to *The Histories of Four-Footed
Beasts*.[57] Finally, attention to nature and its spiritual significance
was a way of occupying the mind with holy things. Theologians
were mindful that (as Thomas Goodwin says) "our thoughts at
best, are as wanton Spaniels"; unguided curiosity might prove
as dangerous to our minds as it had been to Dinah, who wandered away from her family and was raped. Satan is ever eager
to ravish the unwary heart, but one occupied with "holy meditations" is armed against him.[58]

The Latin root of "meditation" means "exercise," "practice,"
"rehearsal." Meditation on the creatures was regarded as therapy
for those weak faculties which are as yet "renewed but in part."
As Edward Reynolds writes in an early "psychology," *A Treatise
of the Passions and Faculties of the Soule of Man*, "Education, then,

and Custome, doe, as it were, revenge nature," and to "revenge nature," that is, man's fallen state, is the Christian's work on earth.[59] To hope for the "spiritual discernment" of an unfallen Adam is futile—man can never regain the ease that he had displayed in naming the animals, "out of the plenty of his own divine wisdome . . . as it were out of a Fountaine of prophesie."[60] This ability, which is closely akin to the poetic power, was lost with Eden; but with justification, the process of restoration begins. As Goodwin writes, "A heart sanctified, and in whose affections true grace is enkindled . . . out of the things he sees and heares, out of all the objects [which] are put into thoughts, he distilleth holy, and sweet, and useful meditations: and it naturally doth it, and ordinarily doth it, so farre as it is sanctified."[61] In terms of Blake's "Proverbs of Hell," the saint does not see the same tree that the lost soul sees.

Protestant meditation on the creatures belongs to the category of "occasional" or "extemporal" meditation. Thus it is distinguished from the models Louis L. Martz uses in *The Poetry of Meditation* in two principal ways: by its object (whatever was apparent to the senses) and by its emphasis on drawing significant analogies with the self.[62] The Christian was trained to find spiritual meaning in all his experiences. For the adept, all consciousness becomes a dialogue between speaking nature and the listening heart, a constant stream of prayer and praise. The structure of extemporal meditation is simple, having three parts: first, observation of the natural scene (a description as minute and evocative as the author's power permits); second, the mind's response, including application to the self, with emphasis on drawing parallels between the meditator's inward self and the rest of creation; finally, a prayer. At the conclusion of his observations about the relationships among the creatures and himself, the meditator is drawn upward towards God. Such meditation may be and ideally *is* occasioned by the smallest details of the creation. Bishop Hall, whose object, he writes, is that the reader "learne how to reade Gods great Booke, by mine," meditates "Upon a faire Prospect," "Upon occasion of a Redbrest comming into his Chamber," "Upon the sight of an humble and patient Beggar," "Upon the Ruines of an Abbey."[63] (The way in which such an attitude points toward a Wordsworthian poetics is evident.)

But the doctrinal foundations of occasional meditation limited
the uses of the practice to two functions. Man might see the
wisdom and power of God, and acknowledge that all things come
from him, at the same time feeling more truly his human insignificance in relation to the divinity; and he might learn a lesson
in morality from the innocent lives of the animals, who exhibit
a loyalty and devotion that put man to shame.[64] The last lesson
the meditator learns is negative: he sees that the world is not
God, nor his own home. As Godfrey Goodman writes, "In our
knowledge of God, the Creatures are not our bounds, but serve
only to point out a Deitie, and then to cry, *Plus ultra, plus ultra,*
and so to leave to God himselfe, sending us from the outward
shop of his works, to the inward schoole of his words, from the
theater of the Creatures, to the sanctuary of his dwelling, there
to learne a new lesson in the knowledge of God."[65]

In the fundamental doctrines of meditation on the creatures,
and the patterns of psychological reaction it encouraged, one
may perceive an important strain in the history of the greater
lyric. Meditation on the creatures, with its constant emphasis on
the analogies between subject and object, on emotional response
and its sacred significance, lent a new dignity and scope to the
nature lyric. The topographical poem, which Dr. Johnson cred-
ited to John Denham's invention, conforms to this fundamental
experiential pattern. "Cooper's Hill," written in 1647, is good
evidence for the rapid assimilation of theological attitudes into
secular poetic practice. Almost two centuries would intervene
between Denham's poetry and the supreme examples of the
genre, such as *Tintern Abbey*—centuries of unceasing experimentation—but in Wordsworth's poem one finds essentially the same
structure (minute description of the landscape, a search for its
significance to the self, a final turning outward—not to God,
however, but to mankind). Furthermore, in this context one may
see that a belief in the power of baptized imagination to perceive
paradise as "a simple produce of the common day" has clear
antecedents two centuries earlier.

Horace Walpole commented that the architect William Kent's
great discovery was that he leapt the fence and discovered that
all nature is a garden. The attitudes toward nature inculcated
by, among other things, two centuries of Protestantism, led the
poets to a similar discovery—they looked about and saw that all

nature is a poem, God's text. Further, the established meditative
structure constituted a pattern for organizing perceptions and
responses to the order and beauty of this virtually infinite res-
ervoir of themes. The meditative structure was congenial to the
lyric mode; it brought new revelations about the self and about
the relationships between subject and object. Yet this model accounts for one kind of natural experience; for nature is not
always peaceful, it does not necessarily encourage one to fix his
eye on a single sparrow, and thus contemplate the wisdom of
God. For just as God has his wrathful aspect, nature has its
tempests, volcanoes, and thunder. What could these experiences
teach?

The Example of Job

According to traditional, orthodox theology, the justice of God
is a matter of revelation and of faith, not to be apprehended by
reason in this world. Yet the Bible also contains an example of
speculation about the justice of God from the merely human
perspective: the Book of Job. This work asks why the virtuous
should suffer. Having lost everything—family, wealth, health—
Job searches to understand the causes of his dreadful losses.
"Surely I would speak to the Almighty, and I desire to reason
with God," he exclaims (13:3). Though the biblical narrator tells
us that Job's trials are a test devised by Satan, the narrative point
of view is almost entirely limited to that of Job and his companions. Thus the ways of God, the power of God, the nature of
God are presented in terms of human experience, which is primarily experience of God's creation. And finally in these same
terms God answers from the whirlwind, affirming Elihu's admonition that Job's desire to understand the cause and effect of
divine purpose is misguided, and presumptuous—an argument
again founded on experience, though experience heightened by
inspiration: "Hearken unto this, O Job: stand still, and consider
the wondrous works of God" (37:14).

God's speech is an overwhelming account of the grandeur and
plenitude of nature, cast in a series of unanswerable questions
about the nature of things and man's place in the universe. The
divine tone is somewhat sarcastic, that of a long-tried school-
master with an exceptionally dull class:

> Who *is* this that darkeneth counsel by words
> without knowledge?
> Gird up now thy loins like a man: for I will
> demand of thee, and answer thou me.
> Where wast thou when I laid the foundations
> of the earth? declare, if thou hast understanding.
>
>   (Job 38:2–4)

The speech continues for four chapters, and its effect is to
discredit human attempts to "reason," to "understand" the purposes of divine Providence. Job's response is to concede the
inadequacy of human reason, an admission which nevertheless
assumes the validity of experience as a source of human faith:

> I [have] uttered that I understood not; things
> too wonderfull for me, which I knew not.
> . . . .
> I have heard of thee by the hearing of the ear:
> *but now mine eye seeth thee.*
> Wherefore I abhor *myself,* and repent in dust
> and ashes.
>
>   (Job 42: 3, 5–6; my emphasis)

Though God has explained nothing, since his answer is that man
can never *understand,* Job's doubts are nevertheless resolved in
his recognition, through experience, of ineffable mysteries.

Such a shift from reason to faith—from the intellectual to the
emotional, from mediated experience to imagination—is the psychological structure of all theodicies, of all arguments about the
justice of God and the good and evil of our mortal state. Despite
the scholarly discussions, in the seventeenth and eighteenth centuries, of Job as a drama, this narrative is essentially organized
according to the lyric mode as I have defined it. The plot is a
psychological one; the events, Job's loss and suffering, are far
less crucial than his desire to understand them, which defines
the goal or *telos* of the work. An actual staging of the Book of
Job would be as static as a performance of *Samson Agonistes.* The
resolution of the book depends upon Job's final recognition and
acceptance, a psychological transformation. But the Book of Job
is particularly important to the history of the greater lyric because of its source of reconciliation, awe in the contemplation of
sublime nature. This conclusion exemplifies a response comple-

mentary to that encouraged in the practice of meditation on the creatures—a paradigm for answering ultimate philosophical questions through experience.

Until the Reformation, the speech from the whirlwind—and indeed all the book's many references to nature—were read allegorically. Gregory the Great's *Morals on the Book of Job* dominated medieval commentary; Gregory declares that God's description of nature really concerns the founding of the church, and that the animals mentioned are symbolic. Behemoth represents Satan, Leviathan is a figure for pride, and so on. In Gregory's reading, the speech still demonstrates God's absolute government and immeasurable power, but it does not do so by forcing Job to experience the sublimity of the creation.

Aquinas (with many references to Gregory) wrote the only other major commentary on Job during the Middle Ages, and the story of Job was not particularly prevalent in vernacular literature. But with Protestantism came a change both in the interpretation of Job and its presence in the literary consciousness. Predictably, the Protestant reading was markedly different from patristic exegesis. Calvin was apparently fascinated by Job, for his commentary is a folio volume of some eight hundred pages in double columns of type.[66] In it, he elaborates on the spiritual importance of man's experiences with nature, a point briefly treated in the *Institutes,* for of course Calvin takes the many references to nature as literal descriptions. His disciple, Theodore Beza, remarks in his own commentary on Job, "I omit that custome which hath continued ever since *Origines* times, I say not of investing the naturall sense of the sacred text to the framing of certain strange allegories."[67]

Commenting on the various arguments from nature, Calvin stresses that events in the natural world have a personal significance in the lives of the elect, whether to punish, admonish, or reward. He emphasizes that though the voice from the whirlwind may be a voice of wrath, yet God also sends the "sweete showers" which make us feel his favor and "to know him our father and savior, and the partie that nourisheth us." Thus,

> We may on the one side be taught to feare him,
> and to walk in his obedience: & on the other side
> rest ourselves upon him, seing we have so faire

> recordes of his love. . . . *We see then that God's*
> *justice, goodness, and wisdome must be linked with his*
> *almightinesse.*[68]

The burden of Job, as read in the late seventeenth century, was that the ultimate questions of divine justice and providence may be apprehended in feeling, if not through reason, and that nature, in which God accommodates himself to man, offers experience leading to an intuition of that truth which reason cannot comprehend.

Earlier in the seventeenth century, when theology was so explosive an element in the English civil war, Job appeared primarily as an example of patience to those who thought themselves afflicted on every side.[69] But the Protestant reexamination of the text also led to the discovery that the Hebrew original is metrical. Symon Patrick, bishop of Ely, remarks in his popular commentary on Job (1678) that the poetry has a "grandeur [that] is as much above all other poetry, as thunder is louder than a whisper," a remark quoted by Edward Young in the introduction to his own paraphrase.

By the beginning of the eighteenth century, verse paraphrases, particularly of the speech from the whirlwind, abounded. The King James translation was dismissed by one clergyman as "the dust inglorious of prose,"[70] and a lively debate was conducted as to which English verse form might best suit the original. "Pindaricks," heroic couplets, and blank verse were all championed.[71] And another debate focused on a question which only a literal reading of the text could raise: Was Behemoth an elephant or a hippopotamus, Leviathan a crocodile or a whale?

Edward Young's notes to his paraphrase (1719) suggest the elements that such poets found most appealing in the task of paraphrasing the speech from the whirlwind. He writes, "My author accurately understood the nature of the creature he describes and seems to have been a naturalist as well as a poet." And when Young explains what he means by "paraphrase," we recognize that the passage is in fact apparently valued as a kind of physico-theological sermon from the mouth of God himself: "I have omitted, added, transposed," writes Young. "The mountain, the comet, the sun, and other parts, are entirely added: those upon the peacock, the lion, &c. are much enlarged."[72]

Job is also one of the biblical texts Sir Richard Blackmore selected as a model for English poetry in his campaign to restore the art. "I know 'tis said," he writes, "that the Christian Scheme of Religion is not so well accommodated to Poetical Writings, and therefore our Poets are obliged to embellish their Works with the Pagan theology. A wretched apology!" In Job, Blackmore continues, poets have "An Original ... [with] a sublime Stile, elevated Thoughts, magnificent Expressions where the Subject requires them, and great richness and abundance throughout the whole, without the Aids of a Pagan System of Divinity."[73]

As a model for the greater lyric, Job retains its force throughout the eighteenth century. It taught the recognition through nature of human frailty in the face of divine power, a recognition that carried with it an assurance of ultimate order and providence. In the face of such power, man's proper response is awe and humility: Young concludes his paraphrase, "Man is not made to question, but adore."[74] According to the aesthetic categories codified by Burke around the middle of the eighteenth century, Job is the prototype of a man who has experienced the sublime, just as the meditator apprehends Burke's category of the beautiful—order, harmony, a sense of relationship between perceiver and perceived. By the middle of the century, passages from Job had been incorporated into Smith's popular edition of Longinus.[75]

But Job also inspired the poet who would proclaim the grandeur of nature—for meditation on divine power, or sublimity, is a psychological impossibility according to these same aesthetic theories. Not only does Job, the protagonist, learn of that grandeur; the book also hints that the young may be equally inspired, that attitude as much as experience is crucial.[76] Elihu is the youngest of Job's companions, and speaks last, and he speaks out of more than experience, for his argument is confirmed by the speech from the whirlwind. This is experience heightened by inspiration:

> I *am* young, and ye *are* very old; wherefore I
> was afraid, and durst not shew you mine opinion.
>   . . . I said, Days should speak, and multitude
> of years should teach wisdom.

> But *there is* a spirit in man: and the inspiration
> of the Almighty giveth them understanding.
> Therefore I said, Hearken to me. . . .
>   (Job 32: 6–8, 10)

Thus, here in the Book of Job was a model for the prophet of
nature, as well as for the ordinary Christian's response to natural
sublimity. And to the poet the book implied that sublime nature
suggested a path to inspiration and truth.

THE TWO VOICES: PENSEROSO AND PROPHET

Although the lyric mode was for the poet relatively free of the
anxieties of influence, and though the Protestant tradition both
impelled him to regain his lost honor and to return to the pure
springs of lyric—the lyric poetry of praise—still this mode raised
other difficulties unique to itself. As I suggested in chapter 1,
the lyric poet may choose among a variety of voices, ranging
from the absolute impersonality of the primitive lyric, to the
pure, personal style characteristically affected by the Romantics,
to the creation of dramatic characters at varying distance from
the implied poet. The voices which the poets of a particular era
characteristically choose afford a significant way of distinguishing among lyric styles.

The question of voice is a problem for the lyric poet inherent
in the "manner of imitation" itself—one person speaking. Unless
that speaker is endowed with a special authority, he is limited by
his means of knowledge and experience; he may articulate with
great accuracy and insight his own experience, but his capacity
to know truth beyond that is theoretically always in doubt. In
this dilemma one may see the roots of sincerity as an ideal, a
quality by which the speaker convinces the audience that he is
telling a truth worth hearing—but this ideal as conscious criterion was to emerge somewhat later. And when assuming the
traditional stance of the "greater lyric" poet—that of the prophet
or bard—how might the speaker guarantee that his readers would
accept him as a true rather than a false prophet?

As we have seen, there were two voices with biblical and doctrinal authority. One was the meditative voice, that of the sensitive perceiver of nature, who speaks out of that accumulated
wisdom usually acquired by quiet, careful meditation upon the

Book of the Creatures. The other was the man who speaks through divine inspiration, and from experience that goes beyond the ordinary bounds of human knowledge. Such understanding might avoid the bewilderment of appearances and penetrate to the truth by means of intuition, if not by means of human reason or knowledge alone.

A definitive characteristic of the greater lyric in the eighteenth century is that poets rely upon these two voices. And their choice is affirmed, if not determined, by one lyric work of Milton which echoes throughout the tradition I shall be examining. Pope's use of "Il Penseroso" in his most lyrical of works (*Eloisa to Abelard*) is by no means idiosyncratic. I do not wish to argue that "Il Penseroso" is a "source" in the sense that we usually intend the term; instead, it may be seen as an early and concise embodiment of the same cultural and theological assumptions I have enumerated. But if literary critics were trained to search the body of English poetry for types, as exegetes once examined the Scriptures, "Il Penseroso" might well be regarded as a poetic foreshadowing of the eighteenth-century lyric mode.

"Il Penseroso" is a convenient starting point for a number of reasons. It reveals innovations in lyric technique which were eventually to become central in Romantic poetry. Milton's purpose in this lyric (and in the companion piece "L'Allegro") is to portray character by means of definitive activities and objects perceived, using external things to objectify and reveal internal realities. This technique is not in itself new; it is familiar in the allegorical mode, and particularly in Spenser, where landscape is frequently a projection of psychological forces. The crucial Miltonic difference, however, is the shift from the narrative to the lyric mode. That is, the objects perceived are not merely juxtaposed with the consciousness they symbolize; they are also selected *by* that consciousness, and the reader sees them through that perspective. The speaker's perceptions become an index of his mind. Aesthetic experience implicitly defines character.

"Il Penseroso" can therefore be studied as a veritable catalogue of the themes, decor, and subtypes of eighteenth-century lyric poetry as it describes the habits of the meditative man. Such a character seeks out the dim, cool, quiet, and solitary. He prefers to view mankind from afar; he prefers retirement to the city, the nightingale to the lark, study to frolic. His shifting perspectives of nature and of man imply the genres most amenable to this mode of experience: a somber variety of the pastoral ("me Goddess bring / To arched walks of twilight groves, / And shadows brown that Sylvan loves. . . . Where the rude axe with heaved stroke / Was never heard the nymphs to daunt"); the lyric itself ("Such notes, as warbled to the string, / Drew Iron tears down *Pluto's* cheek / And made Hell grant what Love did seek"); the topographical poem ("Oft on a Plat of rising ground, / I hear the far-off Curfew sound"); the tragedy, the romance, and even the graveyard meditation.

Most significant, however, is the implication that while the happy man's life is ritually repetitive (he ends one day only to begin another), the meditative man's life has a linear, ascending structure; his life is a pilgrimage toward heaven. A life spent in meditation leads to prophecy:

> And may at last my weary age
> Find out the peaceful hermitage,
> The Hairy Gown and Mossy Cell,
> Where I may sit and rightly spell
> Of every Star that Heav'n doth shew,
> And every Herb that sips the dew;
> Till old experience do attain
> To something like Prophetic strain.

"Spell" means "teach"; and "prophecy," in seventeenth-century English, held not only its current sense of foretelling the future or of seeing "things unknown to human sight," but also simply the sense of "preaching." (One Protestant textbook on the composition of sermons was called *The Arte of Prophesying*.)[77] Milton was articulating the principle that was important in contemporary doctrine about the value of meditative experience to the growth and development of the Christian soul on earth.

"Il Penseroso" shows that the meditative man and the prophet may be two sides of the same personality. And each is invested with a peculiar authority, because in this mode of life the highest reaches of human knowledge are attainable. Whether or not Gray and Goldsmith, Thomson and Wordsworth, had this Miltonic model in mind as they wrote, their assumptions, their poetic voices, were formed by the same traditions. Thus Milton's terms may serve as shorthand for the characteristic voices of the eighteenth-century tradition of the greater lyric. These poets invariably choose the voice either of the meditative man or the prophet, sometimes a combination of the two (especially in the more complex lyrics which appropriate the larger traditional genres such as the epic and the tragedy.) Such voices enable the lyric poet to speak with sincerity and authority of his own experience, of his fellow man, and of the ineffable but keenly felt (because directly experienced) principles of order and harmony in the universe.

Poetic Form: "Something Like *Pindarick* Strain"

Still another newly perceived rationale for the lyric mode created a technical dilemma for the would-be lyric poet in the waning years of the Renaissance. The classical tradition to which he looked back had placed most lyrics low on the scale of genres for the same reasons that Protestantism had tended to exalt them—they were intimate and private, personal, particular. And the subjects most compelling, such as the individual response to the natural world, were at once private and as vast as nature itself. The new scholarship revealed that the biblical models were poetry, but of a kind very different from the classical varieties writers had been taught to admire. The classical tradition did offer, however, one resource—the Pindaric ode. Its English rebirth in the mid-seventeenth century was a further concomitant to the rise of the lyric.

Lewalski speculates that the religious lyricists whom she discusses were reluctant to imitate the greater lyric forms of the classical tradition, which though worthy of their high themes, had, it could not be forgotten, been employed in the praise of pagan gods.[78] I suspect, however, that experimentation with the brief lyric modeled on the psalms was simply more amenable to these poets' conception of the intimate and private nature of the soul's intercourse with God. Certainly this prohibition was not universally felt even among "religious" poets; Cowley, who is primarily responsible for awakening interest in the Pindaric ode, wrote his "Pindaricks" on such themes as "The Resurrection" and "The XXXIVth Chapter of the Prophet Isaiah."

Enthusiasm for the Longinian model well before the turn of the eighteenth century suggests that in the writing of greater lyrics, as in the preoccupation with the sublime, classical sources became suddenly appealing because their forms, and the au-

thority for their themes and techniques, were already interesting
for other reasons. Samuel H. Monk, one may note, assumes in
his influential work *The Sublime* that interest in this aesthetic
begins with the explosion of interest in Longinus in the 1720s.
But as Marjorie Nicolson suggests in her discussion of "New
Philosophy" in *Mountain Gloom and Mountain Glory,* "*The Sublime*
had come to England well before the rhetorical theories of Longinus began to interest Englishmen."[79] The most far-reaching
result of the new fashion of writing Pindarics, however, is to be
found not so much in the many odes produced during the eighteenth century, as in certain ideas which Pindaric odes forced
upon poets' consideration concerning the relation between poetic form and content. For the Pindaric ode recognized a principle of order that is internal, a function of each work's content,
rather than a priori or externally fixed.

In the development of the greater lyric, the classical model
appears to have been a secondary force: the Pindaric ode began
to interest English poets in the late seventeenth century because
it was a workable paradigm for "greater lyrics" flexible enough
to accommodate the vast reaches of nature and of mind. A hint
that this is the primary order of cause and effect is Trapp's
speculation that Pindar himself must have been indebted to the
Bible. Asserting that the chief property of lyric poetry is "that
it abounds with a Sort of Liberty which consists in Digressions
and Excursions," a freedom then usually associated with Pindar,
he continues:

> not that he [Pindar] is to be esteem'd the Inven-
> tor of it: For it is plain that he, and the rest of
> the *Grecians,* receiv'd their Learning from the
> Nations of the East, the *Jews* and *Phoenicians:*
> And it is well known, the eastern Eloquence
> abounded not only with Metaphors, and bold
> Hyperboles, but in long Digressions; as is suf-
> ficiently evident from the sacred Writings.[80]

Cowley describes his efforts at Pindaric translation and imitation in this way:

> I am in great doubt whether they will be under-
> stood by most Readers; nay even by very many
> who are well acquainted with the common Roads

> and ordinary Tracks of Poesie. . . . The Digres-
> sions are many and sudden, and sometimes long,
> according to the fashion of all Lyriques, and of
> Pindar above all men living. The Figures are
> unusual and bold, even to Temeritie, and such
> as I durst not have to do withall in any other
> kinde of Poetry.[81]

One of Cowley's Pindaric imitations is called "The Resurrection," which reveals his sense of the form's thematic possibilities; clearly an important source of its appeal was the accommodation it afforded for great sacred themes. One of Job's paraphrasers also ventured on "Pindaricks" (with unhappy results). He begins:

> In that fam'd Quarter of the world, the East,
> Where light expiring in th'*Atlantick* Main
>   So gloriously revives again,
> The *Uzzites* a large tract of ground possest,
> And here lived Job among the rest. . . .[82]

The freedom of the Pindaric style, however, evoked the most interest and comment. Dryden writes that "the *Pindarique* Verse allows more Latitude than any other . . . the seeming easiness of it, has made it spread. . . . It languishes in almost every hand but [Cowley's]"[83] For Norris "the *Pindarick* is the highest and most Magnificent kind of Writing in Verse, and consequently fit only for great and noble Subjects, such as are as *boundless* as its own Numbers."[84] Sprat writes in his *Life of Cowley* that "the Pindarick . . . by reason of the *Irregularity* of its *Numbers* . . . makes that kind or *Poesie* fit for all manner of Subjects: for the *Pleasant,* the *Grave,* the *Amorous,* the *Heroick,* the *Philosophical,* the *Moral,* and the *Divine.*"[85] "Variety" was another source of pleasure attributed to the Pindaric. "The frequent alteration of the *Rhime* and *Feet,* affects the Mind with a more various delight, while it is soon apt to be tir'd by the settled pace of any one constant Measure," declares Sprat.[86] And this pleasurable variety seemed to lend the form a special facility for the "imitation" of the passions.

One can appreciate the energy with which Pindaric imitations and biblical subjects were taken up (and also sympathize with Dryden's comment that few indeed could use the form with skill) simply by examining the table of contents in early anthologies

of poetry, such as Chalmers's multivolume collection published
in 1810. Works written in the late seventeenth century include
these titles: by Roscommon, "A Paraphrase on the Cxiith Psalm,"
"Ode on Solitude," "The Dream," "On the Day of Judgement";
by Pomfret, "Upon the Divine Attributes: A Pindaric Essay,"
"Eleasar's Lamentation over Jerusalem," "A Pindaric Ode: On
Christ's Second Appearance to Judge the World"; by Waller, "Of
Divine Love: A Poem in Six Cantos," "On the Fear of God, in
Two Cantos," "Of Divine Poesy: In Two Cantos, occasioned upon
the sight of the 53rd chapter of Isaiah Turn'd into Verse by Mrs.
Warton," "On the Foregoing Divine Poems."[87]

One might safely wager a considerable sum that in such an
anthology the poems patently aspiring to the lyric mode during
the period with which we are concerned far outnumber all others. Few have much poetic merit. But this new taste for the
Pindaric, with its exciting glimpses of freedom and sublimity,
also raised new difficulties for the critic. How was one to judge
a poem which created its own rules, having no regular meter,
no fixed form? Trapp points out that such compositions "seem
to avoid all Method, and yet are conducted by a very clear one;
which affect Transitions, seemingly, without Art, but, for that
Reason, have the more of it."[88] Yet he does not explain how that
method might be determined, and this dilemma remained a
bewildering one for decades. Edward Young's Preface to "Ocean:
an Ode" (1728) is a collection of all the truisms then current
about lyric poetry and this abiding critical dilemma:

> The ode, as it is the eldest kind of poetry, so it
> is more spirituous, and more remote from prose
> than any other, in sense, sound, expression, and
> conduct. Its thoughts should be uncommon,
> sublime, and moral; its numbers full, easy, and
> most harmonious; its expression pure, strong,
> delicate, yet unaffected, and of a curious felic-
> ity beyond other poems; its conduct should be
> rapturous, somewhat abrupt, and immethodical
> to a vulgar eye. . . . Fire, elevation, and select
> thought are indispensable; a humble, tame and
> vulgar ode is the most pitiful error a pen can
> commit. . . . And as its subjects are sublime, its
> writer's genius should be so too.[89]

Perhaps the most significant aspect of the fascination with Pindaric models, however, is that it introduces into the critical consciousness and lyric tradition the idea that form and content can be so intimately related that one is merely an aspect of the other, and that the *way* a subject is treated determines the poem's proper form. Coleridge was to elaborate this principle under the notion of "organic unity," but such a philosophical formulation of it was still remote in 1700. Yet it is not fanciful, perhaps, to see its adumbration in Sir William Temple's statement that certain "poetic" values transcend any rules of decorum: "When I speak of Poetry, I mean not an Ode or an Elegy, A Song or a Satyr . . . but a just Poem."[90] (And soon Pope's *Essay on Criticism* recognized "a grace beyond the reach of art.")

Although the Pindaric ode remained an important genre in its own right throughout the eighteenth century and served as a distant model for some of the highest achievements of Romantic poetry, still the early zeal for the form suggests something deeper—a growing recognition that the subjects and technique of the lyric, particularly the greater lyric, demand a scope, a versatility, and a freedom not felt to be comfortably accommodated by traditional forms, and that the poet must be free to shape the poem according to principles of his own devising. "Odes," wrote Trapp, "begin and end abruptly, and are carried on thro' a Variety of Matter with a sort of divine *Pathos* above Rules and Laws, and without Regard to the common Forms of Grammar."[91]

Such "rules" may compel sympathy with Wordsworth's later description of the sonnet as a safe refuge for the poet who has "known the weight of too much liberty." For the moment, however, in the early years of the eighteenth century, the Pindaric model opened dizzying vistas. But Temple concludes with a judgment that the reader of these Pindaric experiments must surely endorse: "after all I have said [about the requisite faculties of the good poet] 'tis no wonder there should be so few that appeared in any Parts or any Ages of the World, or that such as have should be so much admired, and have almost Divinity ascribed to them and to their Works."[92]

4

Early Flourishes of Prophetic Strain
The Seasons and *Night Thoughts*

If the brief but enormous popularity of Thomson's *The Seasons* and Young's *Night Thoughts* is a valid index, the early eighteenth-century reading public was already showing an eager taste for a proto-Romantic lyricism. These two poems, fairly undistinguished as poetry, are yet instructive in their comprehensive if sometimes awkward assimilation of the themes, the poetic principles, and the assumptions I have traced. Despite their great length and epic pretensions, both works are virtual if somewhat anomalous lyrics. The action of each takes place, as Martin Price has remarked, in "the theater of the mind."[1] Each presents itself as the meditations of one person; perhaps the most interesting observation about this device is that it was chosen at all, which was presumably because the authors assumed it to be a suitable and poetically effective "manner of imitation." Both poems are also in some sense deliberate lyric revisions of *Paradise Lost*, insofar as both are theodicies proposing to justify the ways of God to men. Thomson's and Young's speakers, however, proceed without benefit of Urania or of any other muse. In these "experiential epics" the speaker uses only the resources of mind and nature, of mind *in* nature; from this dialogue some philosophy is derived. Thus one may also understand these poems as Miltonic in another way, as enormous expansions of "Il Penseroso," *The Seasons* elaborating on the process described in my epigraph, *Night Thoughts* on the briefly described nocturnal musings of Milton's speaker.

To a twentieth-century sensibility, *The Seasons* (1726–30) is likely to be the more satisfying of the two works. Like *The Prelude*, it traces the emergence of a prophet from a penseroso by means of a selectively dramatized experience with nature. The consciousness of the speaker is barely individualized, and *The Seasons* can hardly be called autobiographical: one is not tempted to call the organizing consciousness "Thomson." Instead, it seems to be some such collective or generalized entity as "the highly civilized early eighteenth-century mind." (Might the speaker of Eliot's *The Waste Land* be our century's counterpart?)

Given the scope of this project, Thomson faced almost insuperable structural problems. Though the progress of the seasons provides one aspect of poetic structure (temporal but not really narrative), it relates only to the "objective" dimensions of the work; another structural principle was needed for the primary, subjective dimension, the speaker's responses and perceptions in relation to the evolving natural scene. What Thomson develops here as both a local or episodic and a comprehensive pattern of order is the meditative structure that was to be paradigmatic in poetic practice for two centuries: description/meditation/conclusion. The poem's shape as a whole is that of a vastly extended "meditation on the creatures"—the immediate ancestor for this durable poetic form.

As an illustration of how this principle works on a limited scale, one may consider one of Thomson's virtuoso descriptive pieces (perhaps the main source of whatever continuing appeal the poem has today), this one from "Winter"—an eighty-three-line word picture of the course of a storm (118ff.) observed from its inception through its climactic fury to its final subsiding calm:

> In dreadful tumult swell'd, Surge above Surge,
> Burst into Chaos with tremendous Roar,
> And anchor'd Navies from their Stations drive,
> Wild as the Winds across the howling Waste
> Of mighty Waters. . . .[2]   (162–66)

This description is interrupted as the perceiver (or rather imaginer) pauses to reflect: "Let me associate with serious *Night*, / And *Contemplation* her sedate Compeer; / Let me shake off th'intrusive Cares of Day, / And lay the meddling Senses all aside" (205–8). This reflection leads to the expected formulaic drawing of analogies, a reexamination of human life in the light of what has just preceded. The speaker observes that in comparison with the furies of nature's storm, those of the soul ("Vexation, Disappointment, and Remorse") seem paltry and easily tolerable.

This conclusion points the speaker toward the source of both outer and inner tempests:

> Father of Light and Life! thou Good Supreme!
> O teach me what is good! teach me Thyself!
> Save me from Folly, Vanity, and Vice,
> From every low Pursuit! and feed my Soul
> With Knowledge, conscious Peace, and Virtue pure,
> Sacred, substantial, never-fading Bliss!   (217–22)

After this prayer, the speaker resumes his description of the storm which was its ostensible occasion.

The essential meditative structure seen here is not always perfectly exemplified within the poem's main episodes, although there is invariably a rhythm of description-to-meditation-to-conclusion familiar from the practice of meditation on the creatures. Thomson's final purpose behind his observations of nature is still explicitly sacramental. At the same time, he introduces generous and detailed amounts of contemporary scientific lore— reactions to the newly emerged Newtonian physics, speculations inspired by contemporary botanists and zoologists, and the like— which, although still recognizably associated at this time with the traditional meditations upon divine purpose and design, are becoming more and more absorbing for their own sake. It is clear that the descriptive-meditative lyric is showing an increasingly personal and secularized version of the parent strain, thus moving toward the "natural supernaturalism" (with accent on the former) that was the Romantics' characteristic transformation of this tradition.

More interesting, however, is Thomson's broader organization of *The Seasons*. The yearly cycle together with the concluding "Hymn on the Seasons" takes the form of an enormous, multistaged process of meditation. Each book, as I have noted, consists of a number of natural descriptions followed by meditative pauses. At the end of this series, the speaker turns to the significance of each season. "Spring" concludes with musings on "virtuous love," "Summer" with consideration of wisdom and its pursuit through philosophy, which leads him to reflect upon "boundless Love and Perfect Wisdom." Exploration of "Autumn" provokes some reflections on retirement and the blessings of rural life wherein one may live in closest harmony with "nature all-sufficient"; it concludes with a prayer to "Inrich me with the Knowledge of thy works!" "Winter" leads into a summary recognition that in the seasons of nature man sees the image of his own life. All of these lessons may be regarded, however, as preliminary to the conclusion of the "Hymn," in which the speaker realizes that "These, as they change, Almighty Father, these, / Are but the *varied* God!" (1–2). Nature is thus seen as a universal, inescapable manifestation of the divine, an assurance of the wisdom, power, and benevolence of the creator, and the argument from design is given one of its last memorable orthodox statements:

> I cannot go
> Where Universal Love smiles not around,
> Sustaining all yon Orbs and all their Sons,
> From *seeming Evil* still educing *Good*,
> And *Better* thence agin, and *Better* still,
> In infinite Progression.   (111–16)

(One may notice how the traditional theodicy argument concerning evil, here so reminiscent of Pope's formulation in the *Essay on Man*, which is roughly contemporary, also seems to prefigure various nineteenth-century fusions of this argument with a new emphasis upon progress. One sees in Thomson a foreshadowing of Tennyson's *In Memoriam*—a still later attempt to combine theodicy, public meditation, and private lyric on an epic scale.)

Night Thoughts is equally ambitious, and even longer (9,550 lines). This passage from "Il Penseroso" might serve as a gloss for the entire work:

> Let my Lamp at midnight hour,
> Be seen in some high lonely Tow'r,
> Where I may oft outwatch the *Bear*,
> With thrice great *Hermes*, or unsphere
> The spirit of *Plato* to unfold
> What Worlds, or what vast Regions hold
> The immortal mind that hath forsook
> Her mansion in this fleshly nook.   (85–92)

While some portions of the poem's argument reiterate the familiar physico-theological speculations about the purposes and meaning of nature—Thomson's central theme—Young also draws heavily upon other sources, upon recent philosophy and Christian apologetics. Here too, however, the "frame" for such reflections is the experience of one mind. In fact, the fiction that these are the "night thoughts" of one person led many readers (particularly often, as is not surprising, in the nineteenth century) to assume that the work is autobiographical, and to speculate about the identities of "Narcissa" and "Lorenzo." Young encourages such an orientation by remarking in the Preface that "As the occasion of this poem was real, not fictitious, so the method pursued in it was rather imposed by what spontaneously arose in the author's mind on that occasion, than meditated or designed."[3] (A curious mixture of the conventional Renaissance claim for unpremeditated sincerity and the more recently emerged habit of claiming to build truth and wisdom on the foundation of private and carefully specified experiences.) One cannot really claim that Night Thoughts has a lyric structure; it is quasi-formal argument pretending to be free meditation. But the pretense, the ostensible occasion, is that which we increasingly associate with all poetry from this time on; the author's choice of a simulated lyric occasion in itself tells us much about his reader's current generic expectations.

Just as Young's criticism (primarily the Conjectures Upon Original Composition, of 1759, and his various prefaces) remains startling for its extreme Romantic ideas about poetry (far more extreme, it might be said, than Wordsworth's), so Night Thoughts remarkably foreshadows the poetic practice of Wordsworth. The seminal ideas of The Prelude are all there, if not its poetic texture. One finds, for example, the notion of a theodicy of the landscape, and nature's moral signficance for man:

> All evils natural are moral goods:
> All discipline, indulgence, on the whole. . . .
>
> . . . .
>   Thus, in thy world material, Mighty Mind!
> Not that alone which solaces and shines,
> The rough and gloomy challenges our praise.
> The winter is as needful as the spring;
> The thunder, as the sun. . . .   (IX, 390–91; 481–85)[4]

(Obviously, this bears comparison with the famous lines from
The Prelude, Book I, beginning, "Fair seedtime had my soul, and
I grew up / Fostered alike by Beauty and by Fear"—as well as
with numerous other passages.)

In experience of the sublime, Young writes, man feels the
sublimity of his own soul. By contemplating the heaven,

> Not as a stranger does she wander there;
> But, wonderful herself, though wonder strays;
> Contemplating their grandeur, finds her own
> . . . .
> Grows conscious of her birth celestial.   (IX, 1025–27; 1032)

This passage foreshadows Wordsworth's "Apostrophe to Imagination," in Book VI of *The Prelude.* And in recognizing this
visionary power one awakens to the glories of the world:

> Dazzled, o'erpower'd, with delicious draught
> Of miscellaneous splendours, how I reel
> From thought to thought, inebriate, without end!
> An Eden this, a Paradise unlost!
> I meet the DEITY in every view. . . .   (IX, 1068–72)

This premise here both looks backward to the notion mentioned
earlier that the saint's perceptions of nature are sharper and
truer and forward to Wordsworth's "Prospectus."

Night Thoughts is exasperatingly repetitive, and the crucial ideas
appear elsewhere than in the final book. Their appearance supports my contention that there is an important link between early
Protestant doctrine about the creation and some definitive tenets
of Romanticism. Young's poem falls halfway between a traditional theological treatise on the creatures and *The Prelude.* If
ideas about the Imagination were later imported from Germany
(the generally recognized sources of Coleridgean and Wordsworthian theorizing), one can see why they were transplanted,
for native strains of the same type had been flourishing for some
time. In its more elegantly sublime statement of these ideas, in
its combining of natural description and spiritual meditation
within a quasi-epic and narrative poem, perhaps even in its modified use of prayer (Wordsworth's poem is ostensibly addressed
to Coleridge), *The Prelude* probably owes more to Young's poem
than to formal philosophy of any kind. Wordsworth's familiarity

with his countryman and predecessor is certain, and to a sensibility like his this poem would have made as indelible an impression as the Germanic ideas which so engrossed his friend Coleridge. The popularity of *Night Thoughts* and *The Seasons* is long vanished, and presumably this obscurity has discouraged critical emphasis on their status as suggestive models for Wordsworth's lyric-epic on nature and the mind of man.

PART TWO

Lyric Appropriations

5

Satire into Lyric

The Vanity of Human Wishes

The genre of *The Vanity of Human Wishes* has been a secondary but persistent theme in twentieth-century criticism of Samuel Johnson. For a long time any discussion was preempted by Johnson's subtitle, "In Imitation of the Tenth Satire of Juvenal." Imitation, according to Johnson's *Dictionary*, is "a method of translating looser than paraphrase, in which modern examples and illustrations are used for ancient, or domestick for foreign." Certainly in his poem Johnson made such substitutions; even a casual comparison of model and imitation, however, reveals fundamental differences in tone and structure. If the poem is satire, it is hardly Juvenalian, for Juvenal's mocking laughter is replaced by an attitude more akin to pity and fear. Howard D. Weinbrot reads the poem as "satiric affirmation," which attacks vice, praises virtue, and offers man hope. Walter Jackson Bate has called the poem a "satire manqué"; others, implicitly taking into account this fear and pity, have argued that the work is fundamentally tragic. The discussion becomes more complicated if one ponders Ian Jack's comment that its vision is "medieval," Lawrence Lipking's demonstration of its affinities with the allegorical *Vision of Theodore*, its widely assumed kinship to *Rasselas* (a philosophical fable), and still others' illustrations of its continuity with Johnson's essays and sermons. Finally, one comes to T. S. Eliot's apparent praise for a work which has "the virtues of good prose."[1]

This "vanity" is one of Johnson's favorite themes, used frequently elsewhere, but rendered in poetry on this occasion, one surmises, because he wanted to give it the stylized dignity and emotional force that poetry alone can impart. Still, Eliot points to a real peculiarity of the work. *The Vanity of Human Wishes* is for us "unpoetic"—at least in light of most subsequent verse, and even in comparison with such great Augustan predecessors as

Pope. Perhaps its critics have assumed, at least implicitly, that
this poetry somehow does *not* "evaporate in translation," that it
"means" the same whether in verse or prose paraphrase—a genuine "poetry of statement," if such poetry exists. But this assumption is misleading, for in terms of statement alone the poem
appears fundamentally disunified. As Damrosch remarks, "One
cannot claim too subtle an interrelation of parts. *The Vanity of
Human Wishes*, even more than Juvenal's tenth satire, is a very
miscellaneous poem."[2]

Indeed, citing various examples of mankind bewildered in
"the clouded maze of fate" (6), the speaker of the poem moves
seemingly at random, indiscriminately, between past and present, mixing historical figures and types: Wolsey and Charles of
Sweden coexist with the ambitious belle and scholar, with Xerxes
and the aged man.[3] Nor does the concluding resolution to these
reflections upon the human condition necessarily follow in any
rational or logical sense. It follows instead in terms of a logic of
feeling, and then only if one shares the speaker's coherent world
view which remains implicit until the final twenty lines, disguised
by the subtitle encouraging us to read the poem in the context
of classical satire rather than in that of Christian stoicism. Johnson (like Marvell in "To His Coy Mistress" or Donne in "A Valediction: Forbidding Mourning") depends ingeniously upon the
appearance of reason rather than upon reason itself.

Corollary to this deliberate but subliminally felt tension between reason and emotion is that between model and imitation,
and between the two very different ethical systems that they
imply. This entire pattern creates a kind of double vision, a
product of the reader's simultaneous perception of similarity
and difference. Johnson would have assumed, particularly in
light of his explicit direction, that his audience would have the
model in mind as they read; but this perspective has now been
lost for most readers. The resulting impoverishment perhaps
most severely modifies our reading of the poem's ending, where
we encounter a voice that is wholly Johnson's—the last twenty
lines. Here the deliberate departure from Juvenal renders the
poem's perceived structure as a recognizable but clearly modifed
version of the miniature histories first cited: the essential pattern
in both cases is that of an abrupt, unanticipated shift in fortunes

which changes both the direction and the significance of experience.

In this final movement, however, the direction is not downward from prosperity to ruin, but upward, from ruin to restoration. In this shift (which also makes the poem comic in the broad, structural sense) the disjunction between imitation and model has become so great that one may be reminded of the "revisionary ratio" that Harold Bloom has called "Tessera," a "completion and antithesis" of an earlier by a later poem. This ratio occurs, according to Bloom, when "a poet antithetically completes his precursor by so reading the parent-poem as to retain its terms but to mean them in another sense, as though the precursor had failed to go far enough."[4] One hesitates to use Bloom's term because Johnson's revision of Juvenal cannot convincingly be attributed to an unconscious dynamic of poetic anxiety. Nevertheless, it is plausible to suppose that Johnson's revision was a conscious strategy to make his conclusion all the more dramatically affirmative through the implicit comparison with Juvenal. Certainly the "parent" poem has a much less emphatic sense of an ending. Juvenal stops with the comment that "Fortune would not be a goddess if men did not make her one." In fact, Johnson's revision of this conclusion affirms an earlier eighteenth-century critical truism (argued by Dennis and others) that *Paradise Lost* is a greater epic than Homer's because Milton had had the benefit of Christian revelation. In deliberately calling the reader's attention to his classical model, Johnson is tacitly saying: "Experience confirms Juvenal's picture of human life and human nature; but he could only describe, never resolve, this enduring and hopeless dilemma. We, with our different and mercifully enlightened perspective, can; here is something one indeed may hope for."

Instead of speaking of revisionary ratios, however, a modern critic may prefer to discuss the relationship between the two poems as another fine example of generic blending. In rewriting Juvenal, it seems, Johnson's deepest allegiance was to quite another treatise on the vanity of human wishes, from another tradition: the Book of Ecclesiastes. This work differs from Juvenal more in tone than in content. The contrast lies not in what the speaker sees in his survey of mankind but in what he finally makes of it, and thus in the consequent shape imposed upon his literary expression of that conclusion. The "double vision" I spoke of earlier, concerning the distortion of the model, could equally be applied to the two disparate views of reality created by the speakers of the two poems. Juvenal's classical satire is limited to the earthly; he has no metaphysics. The biblical preacher, however, sees earthly life in the context of heavenly truth—which is one definition of what it is to be a prophet. The mixing of these two, and the emerging triumph of the latter perspective, results in a mode of poetry that might be described as secular prophecy, or as an experiential "greater lyric"—a poem performing the conventional functions of the greater lyric although the speaker claims no final recourse to any authority other than himself and his wide observation, or to any experience beyond the earthly.

No one to my knowledge has noted that the action of this poem is psychological and internal—that the cast of characters is summoned to the bar of memory (which accounts for their historical and ontological diversity), and that the poem ceases when peace of mind is achieved ("With these celestial wisdom calms the mind, / And makes the happiness she does not find"). Hence a strong lyrical element is incipiently present; admittedly, lyricism is an unexpected result in this hybrid of satire and prophecy. And yet, lyricism is a kind of recessive characteristic in each of these "parent" kinds. Satire is akin to lyric in that it presents a vision of reality filtered through the sharply delineated (if rather universalized) mind of the satirist, who perceives only human vice and folly. In criticism we are as accustomed to blurring the distinction between the historical and the implied satirist as we are that between the historical and implied lyric speaker. We also tend to distinguish among varieties of satire according to the personae of the person who originated them—Juvenalian, Horatian, and so on. And the appropriation of satire even into the more private lyric kinds appears occasionally, even in Romantic verse—as in Shelley's sonnet "Lift not the painted veil."[5]

Prophecy also has a long-standing though perhaps not too intimate association with the lyric. Not only was the "greater lyric" assumed to be the vehicle of prophecy; eighteenth-century biblical scholars like Bishop Lowth argued that the Hebrew prophets were best regarded as lyric poets. In an etymological argument reminiscent of Sidney, he writes: "it is sufficiently apparent, that the word *Nabi* was used by the Hebrews in an ambiguous sense, and that it equally denoted a Prophet, a Poet, or a Musician, under the influence of divine inspiration."[6] After giving several examples, Lowth argues further that the association was neither accidental nor inconsequential: "Nor is it reasonable to suppose, that Prophecy admitted Poetry and Music to a participation in the name alone; on the contrary we find that she did not disdain to unite herself with Harmony, and to accept of her assistance."[7]

In Johnson's poem, then, it is as if two recessive traits of the lyric had blended to become dominant, or nearly so. This work gives as specific and experientially colored (though not so private) a view of reality as the "Ode to a Nightingale." Part of its strategy is to suppress any sense of individuality, however, by means of a high level of generality in both language and theme (the speaker is not really looking at or hearing anything). Prophets, after all, should seem to speak from a universal perspective. But in *The Vanity of Human Wishes* we nevertheless hear (as in satire) a distinctive voice, and it articulates a coherent vision of human life which is neither description nor argument. It is close to what Frye has described as the "proclaiming rhetoric" of the biblical prophets.[8] Since the coherence and unity which I am stressing has been disregarded or questioned by critics, however, I shall first indicate some poetic evidence for it.

Johnson praised Shakespeare because he did not allow rigid generic conventions to constrict his portrayal of life, "the real state of sublunary nature," in which good and evil, joy and sorrow, are mixed and coexistent.[9] In *The Vanity of Human Wishes*, although Johnson violates his two models, he does not do so in the interest of giving us a varied and realistic picture of human life. As the speaker shows us mankind from China to Peru through the lens of his moral vision (a magic lens which sees through pretense, appearance, and temporary states), he shows us only the deepest and final truth: though his subjects are varied, they share the same sad fate.

Thus Johnson's poem seeks to fulfill a didactic purpose rather narrower than is typical of the broad vision of human variety sought by Shakespeare, and at the same time different from the Juvenalian purpose of scourging human folly in all its variety.

An understanding of Johnson's distinct purpose, however, demands consideration not only of the "matter" or attitudinal content to which previous criticism has given full and nearly exclusive
attention, but also to the manner, to the work's specifically poetic
dimensions.

The language of *The Vanity of Human Wishes* does not, in spite
of a richly modulated and pervasive irony often associated with
the satiric vision, invite "close reading" of the sort that has become customary since the New Criticism.[10] On the level of diction
it seems so self-effacing a medium of expression as to remind
us of Johnson's ideal, a "stile which never becomes obsolete . . .
which is probably to be sought in the common intercourse of
life, among those who speak to be understood"[11] No doubt this
plain diction is one of the qualities Eliot had in mind when he
ingenuously praised the poem's "prosaic" excellence. Such a
quality has proved deceptive, however: clarity and conversational
directness can be a virtue surprisingly difficult to analyze or to
describe precisely (one thinks also of the relative scarcity of subtle
close readings, at the verbal level, of such poets as Ben Jonson
or A. E. Housman). In the case of Johnson's poem the "prosaic"
plainness has unfortunately led critics to an undue preoccupation with paraphrasable content, and with literary sources acknowledged in ways that do not seem to lead back to the text.
Yet the vaguely felt if powerful authority of this poem is in fact
very largely the product of a complex, unobtrusive metaphorical
harmony from which its view of things seems to coalesce as
vision; or, to preserve my metaphor, its multiplicity of thematic
motifs is heard as one music.

As a suggestive example of how this metaphorical music works,
one may consider these familiar lines:

> There mark what ills the scholar's life assail,
> Toil, envy, want, the patron, and the jail.   (159–60)

This couplet is often quoted mainly because, as every anthology
notes, Johnson substituted "patron" for "garret" after his quarrel
with Lord Chesterfield. Yet reading the lines in the context of
all that has preceded them, one perceives more than the pointed
compactness, the elegant economy of detail. The lines continue,
for one thing, the series of commands to "See," "look," "mark"—
one instance of a unifying motif consisting of the reiterated

suggestion that the speaker is guiding his audience on a tour of earthly experience (which actually turns out to be a kind of Inferno), that he is playing Virgil to our Dante. (The imperative mood of the verbs also implies that the guide speaks to us and invites us to repeat and to confirm for ourselves his own instructive experiences.)

The subject of the relative clause, "ills," appears pedestrian enough, yet it too is but one example from an extensive series; among the innumerable varieties of illness, literal and figurative, physical and psychological, that have already appeared, are "fancied ills" (10), "fatal heat" (17), "fatal sweetness" (18), "wide-wasting pest!" (23), "madded land" (30), "pain" (43), "tainted gales" (46), "maladies" (117), "disease" (130), "fever of renown" (137), "contagion" (138), "opiate fumes" (150), "fatal dart" (151), and "torpid veins" (153). Following this couplet, near the middle of the poem, the fine rain of kindred images will continue.

Or consider the verb "assail." In examining such an apparently casual choice one gains a new respect for the richness and depth of Johnson's response to language; it is as if he experienced words in three dimensions, where most of us feel only two. The conjunction of "ills" and "assail" considered in isolation seems a merely conventional personification. But again, in the context of the whole, the verb evokes as extensive a pattern as does "ills." A synonym for attack, and derived from the Latin "to leap upon," it forms part of a continuous chain of reference to warfare and aggression; there are "strife" (3), "afflictive dart" (15), "fall . . . massacre" (22), "seize" (39), "destroy" (40), "invade" (41), "assails" (45), "piercing gibe" (62), "pierce" (64), "conquest" (107), "seize" (108), "keen" (110), "misfortune's blow" (127), "captive Science," "last retreat" (144), "fatal dart" (151), "invade" (153).

Such examples of telling but unobtrusive verbal resonance could be multiplied almost indefinitely; equally powerful are the subtle varieties of metaphorical patterning, as in this passage:

> Unnumber'd suppliants crowd Preferment's gate,
> Athirst for wealth, and burning to be great;
> Delusive Fortune hears th'incessant call,
> They mount, they shine, evaporate, and fall.   (73–76)

The primary subject here is the satire upon seekers after political power, a familiar theme. But the description is more interesting

than its conventional diction might at first reveal. Because the psychological is expressed in terms of urgently physical, temporary states ("Athirst," "burning"), these aspirants to fame and fortune take on the ephemerality of the unworthy goals they seek. And when, elsewhere, they are aligned implicitly with a vital force of nature (rain), they appear incarnated as insects, creating a figure "mixed" yet congruent in relation to the one already cited. They buzz at Preferment's door like flies on a closed window, they have their brief day in the sun (when Fortune "shines" on them), they disappear, and then in a curious transmutation from one form of matter to another, "They mount, they shine, evaporate, and fall." Fires, flies, and water droplets have all been used before as poetic symbols of the ephemeral, but in magically conflating them into a series, Johnson implies that such ambition is at once one of society's "natural" forces but mercurial, inevitably and quickly perishable.

The intricacy of these metaphorical reverberations creates a thematically pertinent sense of analogy among supposedly distinct entities and thus implies a coherent, perceptually defined consciousness which sees things as a whole rather than as an assortment of isolated parts, a mere catalogue. The metaphorical transformations, moreover, express a universal conflict and an eventual deterioration resulting from the ceaseless friction between human nature (with its ruling passions of hope, fear, desire, hate, pride) and material nature (with its defining principles of conflict, decay, and loss). According to the poem, these earthly "ills" may manifest themselves in mind, in nature, or in society—they may appear as senility, madness, war, treason, execution, failure, loss of beauty or of power or wealth. Quite frequently one of them is denoted metaphorically in terms of another: the Beauty's progress in society is spoken of as a war (319–42). The description of Charles of Sweden's loss resulting from hubris is both literally caused and figuratively imaged in the natural terms of winter and ice.

I must at this point make it quite clear what such verbal patterns have to do with my overall sense of generic experimentation in Johnson's poem and the others examined in this book. In order to appreciate the way in which, as I see it, Johnson is accommodating his classical model and traditions toward assimilation with an increasingly dominant lyric mode, one must note several facts. First, certain "harmonies" of metaphoric repetition and transformation appear to be the chief and perhaps the only principle of formal coherence that emerges through the abundance of apparently random homiletic examples, and reveals them as a unified pattern rather than simply as a catalogue. Second, such unity is not merely "linguistic" or "figurative" but necessarily implies a common center of judgment, feeling, and perception from which the unity of pattern radiates, in short, a consciousness which is the poem's real center. Finally, in the absence of other principles of coherence (narrative lines, "imitated" natural processes, logic), and given also that the poem's concluding resolution is overtly presented as an achieved inner or psychological equilibrium, it is clear that we see here the characteristic shape, if not the fully developed physiognomy, of a lyric poem.

One further realization that emerges from Johnson's subtle patterning of figurative language is a historical one: this analogical way of seeing, with its vast system of correspondences, exemplifies an old and familiar world view. The poem, in doctrinal terms, is "medieval," as Jack has remarked, not only in its tone of *contemptus mundi* but also in its vision of the world as an intricately interrelated structure in which all the parts mutually reflect as well as affect one another. It is also arguably a world of Heraclitean flux, for the imagery pattern I have described evokes a cosmos in which everything tends perpetually toward a paradoxical change-within-stasis. This principle governs both inner and outer reality: matter itself seems as insubstantial as the mist and airy phantoms of man's moral and psychological worlds.

My strategy thus far has been to point out certain limited but pervasive principles of metaphorical continuity which appear throughout the body of Johnson's poem, in the famous survey of mankind. The most difficult question, however, concerns the continuity between this "body" and the conclusion. Given the metaphorical patterns we have observed, it seems reasonable to inquire whether a similar principle might serve as a modulation into the poem's resolution. An important condition to observe is the effect created by this long and apparently most heterogeneous list, which, as we have seen, is fundamentally not so disparate after all.

Johnson's catalogue of examples is long for sound rhetorical
reasons. It is unified both by metaphorical means and by a principle of repetition—each little history has the same shape, a
downward curve, though the particulars continually change. In
this sense the poem resembles a musical theme and variations,
a composition in which the variations are in one or two closely
related minor keys, until the last statement of theme, when the
same material is suddenly transposed into the major. As an argument, therefore, the point is carried not by proof in any logical
sense but by Johnson's implicit pattern of suggestion that, no
matter how long the list is extended, any further examples can
only disclose new variants of the same pattern. His point is less
"thesis" than axiom, a principle that is experientially self-evident
and that can be demonstrated ad infinitum. Experience, he implies, endlessly confirms the theme with which he begins: "hope
and fear, desire and hate / O'erspread with snares the cloudy
maze of fate"; man is forever betrayed by "vent'rous pride."

   Although Johnson reverses Juvenal most pointedly in the conclusion, or because he does so, it is there that the ordering principles of the work emerge most clearly. In the conclusion we feel
the antithesis and the pattern of literary completion that Bloom
discusses; the lines also evoke the most troubling questions about
the poem's degree of unity and integrity. At first they do seem
a rather unseemly boulder to heave into the delicate web that
theme, tone, and richly woven metaphor have created—but then
a thousand Lilliputian threads were able to bind Gulliver, and a
similar principle is at work here.

>   Enquirer, cease, petitions yet remain,
>   Which heav'n may hear, nor deem religion vain.
>   Still raise for good the supplicating voice.
>   But leave to heav'n the measure and the choice,
>   Safe in his pow'r, whose eyes discern afar
>   The secret ambush of a specious pray'r.
>   Implore his aid, in his decisions rest,
>   Secure what'er he gives, he gives the best.
>   Yet when the sense of sacred presence fires,
>   And strong devotion to the skies aspires,
>   Pour forth thy fervors for a healthful mind,
>   Obedient passions, and a will resign'd;
>   For love, which scarce collective man can fill;

For patience sov'reign o'er transmuted ill;
For faith, that panting for a happier seat,
Counts death kind Nature's signal of retreat:
These goods for man the laws of heav'n ordain,
These goods he grants, who grants the pow'r to gain;
With these celestial Wisdom calms the mind,
And makes the happiness she does not find.   (349–68)

With the concluding couplet one principle of order is finally
made explicit: the poem as a whole is a quest—a search which
is finally rewarded. "Enquire" is derived from the Latin *quae-
rere*—to seek. As in many traditional quests, however, the goal
turns out to be something quite different from what was sought.
Worldly happiness is not, after all, of this world. It can be found
only within, never without. But as in the rest of the poem, the
conclusion is supported by an understated yet effective metaphorical configuration. Essentially these concluding lines re-
direct the psychic energies which impelled the search heretofore.
Man is advised to expend all hope and desire on heavenly, not
earthly, objects. Fear and hate are suppressed by a recommendation to "leave to heav'n the measure and the choice." Accompanying this redirection is a transformation of the various
materials of human ambition which have recurred throughout
the early catalogue. All the seekers after wealth pursued one
goal; here we are shown what real "goods" are. Seekers after
power used but one form of petition and supplication which
invariably disappointed; here we learn what kind of plea *will*
bring happiness. Finally, and most important, the sense of perpetual motion implicit in the restless search for happiness, is
stilled. The words "cease," "rest," "secure," and "calm" all point
to the discovery of certitude.
     From this analysis of poetic language, it appears that *The Vanity
of Human Wishes* is much more coherent, and is so by more richly
subtle means, than has usually been assumed; the source of that
coherence is, very largely, a long-ignored associative pattern of
imagery. Such a technique is familiar in other lyrical "arguments"
such as Shakespeare's Sonnet 73 ("That time of year . . ."), Marvell's "To His Coy Mistress," or Donne's "A Valediction: Forbidding Mourning." When we attend also to the emphatic, self-
characterizing tone of the poem's voice, which sharply and significantly distinguishes it from the poetic voice of Juvenal, we

might conclude that the profoundest organizing principle at work is, as stated before, an emergent strain of lyricism—in this case a lyricism well displaced toward the impersonal (see chapter 1), but undeniably present. (Bate, with somewhat different intent, has described the poem as evoking "the inner landscape of [Johnson's] mind.")[12] Located in relation to my topographical schema this poem would be an "impersonal, rhetorical" lyric.

As was made clear in chapter 2, genre classifications are useful mainly for what they may illuminate in a particular work. If my attempts to show some definitive lyric features in Johnson's poem have revealed its structure and its rationale in a new way, then my efforts have been quite fully justified. Whether the poem, all things considered, is finally to be termed "a lyric" is far less important. Perhaps the fairest way to put it would be to observe that there is a strongly cohesive lyrical "field" here, but that something more might be required before we would for purely labeling purposes want to pronounce it a lyric. Noting its real affinities with other lyrics, however, is useful once one has identified precisely what these and its other generic affinities are. The Johnsonian revision of Juvenal's satire necessarily demanded the reshaping of certain materials by a new and palpably distinct consciousness—that of an eighteenth-century "voice of Experience"—even if, recognizing how far this poem is from prototypical lyrics of the Romantic type, we prefer not to call that consciousness "Johnson" (with quotation marks included). In any case, what emerges from the new strain of verse Johnson has produced, is something obviously akin to prophecy.

After commenting on the poem's curious lack of any apparent sense of an audience, Rachel Trickett astutely remarks that The Vanity of Human Wishes is "the kind of utterance that might be prophetic if it were not for the care with which every attitude is presented through the conventions of the time."[13] But this fact is, I think, the most interesting aspect of Johnson's poem in the context of my view of eighteenth-century developments. In every sense except the convention that prophecy is the speech of a biblical personage directly inspired by God, the poem is prophetic. The speaker is implicitly one who shares the human perspective but whose vision can also transcend it. He sees through experiences to the fundamental patterns behind them.

In The Great Code, Northrop Frye suggests that prophecy may

be distinguished from other modes of biblical discourse in terms
of its purpose and voice. It is a kind of *Kerygma*, "proclaiming
rhetoric," "a mixture of metaphorical . . . and concerned [lan-
guage] . . . but it is not an argument disguised by figuration."
We have observed these characteristics in *The Vanity of Human
Wishes*, in its apparent aim to convince by means of a visionary
rhetoric rather than by argument. The prophet, writes Frye, is
a person of "genuine insight" who has "a comprehensive view
of the human situation, surveying it from creation to final deliverance. . . . The wise man thinks of the human situation as a
kind of horizontal line . . . the prophet sees man in a state of
alienation caused by his own distractions, at the bottom of a U-
shaped curve."[14]

This definition seems to me to explain better than any other
exactly what the design and purpose of *The Vanity of Human
Wishes* implies. Certainly the speaker emerges as a person of
"genuine insight" who has a comprehensive view of man and
human life. The survey of mankind from China to Peru implies
a continuous descent into the inferno of human experience, a
movement which abruptly changes direction with the conclusion.
One significant modification, however—and it is at this point
that the meaning of Johnson's conventions is important—is that
according to Frye the prophetic vision is historical. The prophet
sees mankind's position in terms of his origins (a fall), his present
state, and his ultimate salvation. In Johnson, however, the vision
is expressed not in time but in space; the historical sense is
entirely lacking, since there is no attention paid to chronology,
and the survey oscillates between past and present, with present
as the dominant tense. So the final movement which is supposed
to be a turning "upward" (restoration) is here explicitly a turning
inward ("celestial wisdom calms the mind").

It seems, then, that what has occurred is a displacement of the
prophetic mode not only into commonplace "Augustan" language, but also, implicitly, into the realm of purely human experience. Earlier I suggested that the voice of the poem might
be described as "The Voice of Experience." In reading Ecclesiastes one assumes that the speaker's insight is only partially
conditioned by his experience; he was a prophet first. The speaker
of Juvenal's tenth satire draws no broad conclusions as a result
of *his* experience. But in *The Vanity of Human Wishes* prophetic

conclusions are apparently drawn from "the real state of sublunary nature."

Hence we see that, as prophecy, *The Vanity of Human Wishes* is
poised somewhere between the biblical and the Romantic versions of the poet/prophet. The speaker of Ecclesiastes is wholly
impersonal, and though experiencing a unified vision of human
life he makes that vision authoritative not because we are con-
vinced by his personal experience but because we are led to
assume that he is directly inspired by God. Wordsworth explicitly
assumes the role of "prophet of Nature" at the end of *The Prelude,*
a poem which describes his experience as the growth of a poet's
mind. He comes to prophecy through poetry, whereas the biblical
prophet comes to poetry through prophecy. Johnson, too, is
writing a poem prophetic in its aim and its tone; his claims to
authority are implicit in his evocation of models, and in the kind
of coherence revealed by his vision. Yet, significantly, we accept
his voice as prophetic because it is so obviously the voice of
human experience. The tacitly assumed growth which culmi-
nates in this voice is not that of a poet's mind, but that of a man
who speaks with the collective voice of *all* human experience and
does not seek, like Wordsworth, to characterize that experience
in unique and private terms. Still, long and deep observation of
humankind is implied, and by means of it the poetic speaker
has, like Milton's Penseroso, *attained* "to something like prophetic
strain."

6

Elegy into Lyric
Elegy Written in a Country Churchyard

Gray's *Elegy Written in a Country Churchyard* is unique among the poems discussed here, for ever since publication it has been both popular and universally admired. Few readers then or now would dispute Dr. Johnson's appraisal: "Had Gray written often thus, it had been vain to blame or useless to praise him." In the twentieth century we have remained eager to praise, yet praise has proved difficult; although tradition and general human experience affirm that the poem is a masterpiece, and although one could hardly wish a single word changed, it seems surprisingly resistant to analysis. It is lucid, and at first appears as seamless and smooth as monumental alabaster. Its conspicuous virtue is an apparent *absence* of strain, prophetic or otherwise.

Most of the scholarship about the *Elegy* in the past thirty years or so emphasizes its literary and biographical contexts. The New Critics, who did so much to illuminate works as diverse as "The Canonization" and "Sailing to Byzantium," have not been very successful with this poem. Although Brooks included an essay on the *Elegy* in *The Well-Wrought Urn,* it is not among his best; he argues that close attention to irony, paradox, and poetic structure is as indispensable in reading an eighteenth-century poem as any other; he also decides that the final epitaph, the most puzzling structural aspect of the *Elegy,* may not be an "adequate" conclusion.[1]

It is to New Critical procedures that we owe our awareness of the now famous ambiguity in line 93: who is the person addressed as "thee"? If we can answer that question, then we know whose epitaph concludes the poem and can presumably judge its suitability, and its relation to what came before. Early manuscripts show that Gray's first version of the *Elegy* was ten stanzas shorter, and ended with explicitly didactic advice that one should reconcile oneself to obscurity. After observing that the villagers' constricted lives prohibited them not only from great but also from infamous deeds, the speaker (in that version) draws a lesson for himself:

> Hark how the sacred Calm, that broods around
> Bids ev'ry fierce tumultuous Passion cease
> In still small Accents whisp'ring from the Ground
> A grateful Earnest of eternal Peace
>
> No more with Reason & thyself at Strife;
> Give anxious Cares & endless Wishes room
> But thro' the cool sequester'd Vale of Life
> Pursue the silent Tenour of thy Doom.[2]

Most readers would agree that the later published version is, despite the problematic ambiguity, decidedly better poetry; these lines were a lame conclusion. But if the epitaph and narrative stanzas are more satisfying poetically, why do they nevertheless divert the reader's attention so unaccountably from the first-person speaker of the poem's opening lines?

Some have proposed that the epitaph was intended for someone Gray knew, possibly Richard West, and that the change was thus dictated by extraliterary considerations. For others the epitaph celebrates a *poeta ignotus*, or a village stonecutter, carver of the "uncouth rhymes."[3] Alternatively, we may still assume that the epitaph is for Gray himself, or for the speaker of the poem, a persona distinct from Gray. But if so, then why the careful disguise? Brooks claims (I believe correctly) that the speaker "chooses" this epitaph for himself, and most recent critics agree.[4] But the mere identity of this youth is of less importance than the question of how the epitaph contributes to the poetic force of the work.

This is a stubborn, persistent question. Walter Savage Landor considered the epitaph "a tin kettle tied to the tail of a noble dog." As for the rest of the poem, there are several reasons why it should seem as quaint and antique as Warton's "Enthusiast" or Akenside's "Pleasures of the Imagination": its "poetic diction," which post-Romantic readers have been taught to consider "artificial"; its plenitude of platitudes; its marmoreal impersonality; its evocation of the "graveyard school," which is nevertheless so muted that a reader avid for the gothic frisson would do better to seek out Blair or Parnell. Yet the *Elegy* seems to be much more than the sum of its parts (one of Coleridge's criteria for a true poem), as its long durability shows.[5]

This popular masterpiece, while it evokes any number of analogues and related genres, seems to belong to no one of them in particular. Gray called the poem an "elegy," but to the eighteenth-century reader familiar with *Lycidas,* this work would have seemed a considerable departure from the familiar conventions. The poem has often been regarded as quintessential "pre-Romantic" literature, but that is merely to imply that it seems neither Augustan nor Romantic, a historical judgment of little if any use in understanding what the work *is*. Indeed, this label may have proved itself a barrier to understanding the *Elegy*. With it goes the tacit or explicit assumption that the poem is as near in technique to Dryden as to Wordsworth, and consequently that its meaning is embodied, more or less fully, in its statements. This assumption (often quite misleading even in relation to Dryden or others of Gray's immediate predecessors) can plausibly be supported by reference to many near-contemporaries of the *Elegy;* Pope's *Moral Essays,* for example. For we do read, say, "To a Lady: Of the Characters of Women" largely for its witty, elegant aphorisms about human nature; its organizing principle is, to a considerable extent, the discursive or cognitive mode of an essay in verse. Of course the psychology, and above all the social attitudes of the "implied poet," are discernible though unstated, and they contribute much to that poem's characteristic effects. But they do not function as the *logos* or organizing principle in Pope's poem (in other words, that work is not a lyric according to my definition).

The phrase "poetry of statement" (itself deserving of a critical scrutiny it seems never to have received) is much less adequate to the art of Gray's *Elegy*. So long as one's reading (half-consciously influenced, perhaps, by Arnold's famous dictum about Pope and Gray as "classics of our prose") is colored by such a concept, the poem's shape and its way of moving us will remain mysterious. And in that case I. A. Richards's remark that we respond because it "is perhaps the best example in English of a good poem built upon a foundation of stock responses" remains as pertinent a critical evaluation as any.[6] If, however, we read the *Elegy* from an entirely different perspective, looking for intuitive associations rather than arguments or prose rhythms, perhaps the poem's structure and its evocative appeal will begin to explain themselves. The fact is that the *Elegy*, like many such later poetic meditations as "Frost at Midnight," is organized primarily so as to trace the subtle movements of a particularized and precisely located consciousness. Hence the concluding epitaph is intended as a resolution not to any philosophical debate or narrative plot but to a psychological conflict implicit from the beginning: the fear of death and all that it entails, "obscurity" in all senses of the word. The *Elegy*, one might say, is the meditation of an uneasy young man of poetic sensibility who finally buries himself in thought.

A. E. Dyson once briefly compared the *Elegy* with the "Ode to a Nightingale," and a late eighteenth-century literary historian casually referred to Gray's "*Ode* in a Country Churchyard" (emphasis mine);[7] but the consequences of the work's essential lyricism have never been explored. Many of its superficial features tend to divert one from the poem's actual mode of being. There is, indeed, much about the *Elegy* which seems at first to point in quite different directions than those suggested by the concept of lyric: its "Augustan" diction, its stately, regular quatrains, its elegant reformulations of "what oft was thought." Even the term "elegy," for readers now as then, usually connotes the highly ceremonial, public expression of mourning. It would be foolishly parochial to imply that these dimensions are merely unfortunate limitations of a regrettably unlyrical period style, that the *Elegy* is a Romantic lyric manqué, which Gray might have written better had he written later. As I shall demonstrate, the poem's special verbal idiom—far from being at odds with its ethos—is an important, even crucial, vehicle for the restrained and discreet lyricism which makes the poem so hauntingly effective.

Much evidence compels the conclusion that the *Elegy* is, fundamentally, a lyric. If the identity of the youth and the transposition from "me" to "thee" are the most evident ambiguities in the poem, a careful reading discloses other, more delicate instabilities, and they lead one inescapably to the problem of genre. The opening four stanzas alone tell us that there is something unusual, even highly original, in the techniques of this poem, reassuringly conventional though it may be at the level of surface statement. When alerted to these hints, one recognizes that this familiar landscape of the opening stanzas is not a mere set piece in the *ut pictura poesis* tradition; that it reflects (constitutes a "projection" of) a process quite akin to what a later age would call stream of consciousness.

But even before one enters that landscape, the first and most obvious way in which Gray begins to pique our expectations is through the term "elegy." It is at best an imprecise term; in 1712 Trapp wrote that "this Sort of poem was anciently, and from its first Origin, made use of at Funerals, that therefore, of one famous Elegiac Poet upon the death of another, of equal Fame."[8] But Trapp goes on to explain that the genre is not limited to this theme and situation, for elegies often concern love as well as death ("The Connexion between which," he remarks, "it is not my business here to examine.") Nor is the elegy necessarily limited to expressions of sorrow, though those "full of Joy and Triumph," are, he believes "improperly rank'd in the Number of Elegies." The "chief Property is to be easy and soft; to flow in one even current, and to captivate the ear with melody."[9] And of course when we look back to such earlier instances of the "elegy" as those found in Donne, we recognize that we are dealing with a highly flexible generic label, though Trapp's efforts at definition may show that the term, like "sonnet," is in the process of narrowing and stabilizing its accepted meaning.

For Gray the most important antecedent in the elegiac tradition was probably (given its ubiquitous influence throughout the century) Milton's *Lycidas,* which scrupulously conforms to the ancient conventions in theme and style (though it was not, among other things, "soft and easy enough" for Dr. Johnson, who was skeptical both about it and the classical models upon which it drew). The *Elegy Written in a Country Churchyard* abounds with echoes of *Lycidas* and, as we shall see, it has even deeper affinities with "Il Penseroso." But since Gray's poem not only directly alludes to *Lycidas* but superficially appears to share a subject, a theme, and an emotional rhythm (the movement toward reconciliation), let us first consider this glancing reference.

Gray's *Elegy* is certainly one version of pastoral, but seen in the context of *Lycidas* it looks surprisingly plain in its language and relatively free of conventional ornament. In contrast to Milton's, Gray's apostrophes are subdued, and pastoral life as Gray renders it is closer to the accents of realism; its cruelties, for example, are acknowledged. Milton's presiding nymphs and deities have in the *Elegy* faded into mere abstractions, verbal references to human passions—pride, ambition—or else to the impersonal forces to which human life is inevitably subject: "Nature," "dumb Forgetfulness."

In short, one may surmise that the eighteenth-century reader coming upon Gray's *Elegy* for the first time and having *Lycidas* somewhere in his literary consciousness, would have found Gray's poem fresh, natural, and "modern." Dr. Johnson warmly approved, and while he castigated Milton for the use of what he felt were outworn and distractingly artificial conventions, he praised Gray for those images "to which every bosom returns an echo." One might observe that Johnson was applying a standard remarkably close to Wordsworth's of a few years later, that poetry should be written "in the language really spoken by men," and that it should speak to common joys and sorrows.

Thus Gray radically modifies the Miltonic version of elegiac conventions of style; this is not, however, the only literary model that the opening stanzas evoke and evade. Such allusive evocations, in this poem, seem to shift from stanza to stanza, sometimes from line to line; the first familiar echo that would have struck Gray's *au courant* reader, no doubt, is that of the "graveyard school":

> The Curfew tolls the knell of parting day,
> The lowing herd wind slowly o'er the lea,
> The plowman homeward plods his weary way,
> And leaves the world to darkness and to me.

"Curfew," "tolls," "knell," "parting day," all suggest death, and yet the funereal mood is lightened, almost immediately diverted, in the second line toward something quite different: the lowing herd, while mournful perhaps, recall the familiar pastoral conventions, as does the plowman—though he, in retrospect, may be felt to represent common humanity, plodding its way along the journey of life, homeward toward the grave. But his primary function, initially, is to dramatize the speaker's sense of isolation. Of the remaining lines in this stanza, only the last (especially "darkness" and the idea of solitude) picks up the pattern of graveyard imagery.

The second stanza, however, avoids any evocations of death whatever. It restates the sense of the first ("twilight is here, night is coming"), but to entirely different effect:

> Now fades the glimmering landscape on the sight,
> And all the air a solemn stillness holds,
> Save where the beetle wheels his droning flight,
> And drowsy tinklings lull the distant folds;

While the first stanza emphasizes parting, loss, and increasing solitude, the second highlights the emergence, the appearing, of things. As in "Frost at Midnight," where the "strange and extreme silentness" of the winter evening makes audible the tiniest sounds (such as the "owlet's cry"), here the perfect "solemn stillness" allows the speaker to hear even the beetle and the "drowsy tinklings" of the distant flocks, bells quite different from the opening curfew, which indicate the presence of life and bucolic activity. The stanza demonstrates the aroused and sharpened perceptions of the speaker, perceptions that are continually being reformulated.

This comforting pastoral calm is barely established, however, before it is broken by another, more disturbing revision, again introduced by the word "save":

> Save that from yonder ivy-mantled tow'r
> The mopeing owl does to the moon complain
> Of such, as wandering near her secret bow'r,
> Molest her ancient solitary reign.

Here, as the speaker's eyes move from distance to foreground, the poem veers back toward conventional graveyard imagery (along with the phrases of "Il Penseroso"): ivy-mantled tower, mopeing owl, moonlight; and still, in their context, these details are used in an unconventional way. They are designed not to thrill with terror but to imply that the speaker has entered a sacred realm ("secret," "molest"), one in which, as the next stanza reveals, the imagination begins its work. (The moon implies here all that it does in Wordsworth or Coleridge.)[10]

Through stanza 2, the music of the poem has shaped an opening decrescendo, a sense of endings, fadings, dyings; earth grows quieter, darker, lonelier. In this country churchyard, however, the speaker soon discovers that he unexpectedly has company

after all, and the proper subjects for an "elegy." The fourth and
last of the introductory stanzas is the most lively thus far:

> Beneath those rugged elms, that yew-tree's shade,
> Where heaves the turf in many a mould'ring heap,
> Each in his narrow cell for ever laid,
> The rude Forefathers of the hamlet sleep.

Life is infused into the surroundings, however; animate and
inanimate appear as complementary aspects of one whole. The
yew and especially the "rugged elm" are personified in terms
which might just as aptly be used to describe the "rude Forefathers," while "rude" could as well be applied to the trees. Similarly, the turf "heaves" where the dead "sleep" (the first of many
euphemisms for death in the *Elegy*). It is almost as if we were
witnessing the moment before Resurrection. And so we do observe a kind of resurrection, but one subsisting in the imaginative
empathy of the speaker.

This analysis by no means exhausts the riches of these opening
lines; I have said nothing, for instance, about their sounds and
rhythms, obviously a powerful force in the poem. The point I
want to make is that, despite their clarity and verbal simplicity,
these stanzas are unexpectedly complex and are especially subtle
in the multiple generic affinities they suggest. It seems that any
of several rather different poems could follow. And if we test
this impression, we find that in fact three divergent "poems" *do*
follow, intertwined within one another through the subsequent
stanzas: a graveyard meditation, a reflection upon the universal
human desire to be remembered after death, and an elegy proper,
a funeral celebration (as Trapp put it) "on the death of one poet
by another of equal merit." (These three "poems" are reprinted
in the Appendix.)

The first of these is a conventional graveyard meditation on
the theme of human mortality. It is the briefest of the three, and
the most universal in theme. It is the dominant strain in the
opening four stanzas, since most of stanzas 1, 3, and 4 conform
more or less to its conventions. After the speaker pauses to think
of the "rude Forefathers" asleep in their graves, however, this
motif does not reappear until near the end of the *Elegy*, where
this particular movement concludes appropriately with the reading of an epitaph, which itself ends in the conventional reminder

that Divine Love conquers death (a line which several critics have found to be pointless and inconsistent with the rest of the poem).[11]

But like the modifications of elegiac conventions already suggested, Gray's use of this poetic tradition involves some significant changes. "Graveyard" poems ostensibly concern a grave problem, death, and are an eighteenth-century embodiment of the *memento mori* tradition—the verse equivalent of that tomb sculpture prominent in the late Middle Ages, where the body of the interred was portrayed in a state of partial decomposition. And yet, though the conventions demanded that such poems conclude with a comforting reminder, "Death, thou shalt die," and with an apocalyptic vision of the Last Day, one suspects that the popularity of these poems was due above all to that human proclivity which makes twentieth-century audiences so relish horror movies: the pleasure of being frightened by the gruesome but slightly artificial.

In the usual graveyard poem, most of the poet's lines and energies are directed toward creating as many sublime thrills as possible. And so in comparison with a representative work of this genre, Blair's "The Grave" (1743), Gray's handling of the conventions appears remarkably decorous, even tame. Blair's "wan, cold moon" becomes a simple "moon," "night's fowl bird," a "mopeing owl," and though Gray alludes to the yew-trees, he avoids imagining the grim horrors this graveyard dweller might have observed. In Blair's poem, the yew is an opportunity for virtuoso elaboration:

> Cheerless, unsocial plant! that loves to dwell
> Midst skulls and coffins, epitaphs and worms. . . .   (22–23)

Gray, in fact, avoids the word "grave," preferring the euphemisms "narrow cell," or "lowly bed"—the blunt fact appears only in the metaphorical, aphoristic reminder that "The Paths of Glory lead but to the Grave."

This first of the three principal strands woven into the fabric of the *Elegy* concerns the universal human fate, death, recognized by means of its sign, the grave, that "house appointed to all living" (Blair's epigraph from the Book of Job); but Gray's treatment of the theme is muted, discreet, almost evasive; what is most significant, he avoids any effort to express or arouse terror, the hallmark of the tradition he evokes.

The second "poem," which one might name "A Meditation on
the Universal Human Desire for Earthly Memorials," is corollary
to the first theme, the universality of death. Even here, in this
country churchyard filled with the poor, the humble, the obscure,
the speaker notices the gravestones, "with uncouth rhymes and
shapeless sculpture decked." In this "poem" Gray's emphasis is
upon the universal truth which these tombs mutely suggest: we
all desire to be remembered, and each of us is reluctant to leave
the warmth and light of human sympathy. These, like all tomb-
stones, implore "the passing tribute of a sigh."

The speaker of the poem knows the memorials of the rich
and great as well; they have, perhaps, heroic deeds to record.
But noting this same impulse in the poor, whose annals are "short
and simple," he is led to one conclusion: if these folk share with
the rich a desire to be remembered, they also share the pathos
of that desire. All memorials are "frail"; the storied urn and
animated bust cannot revive the dead. "Flattery" *cannot* "soothe
the dull, cold ear of death." Hence mankind is united not only
by the inevitability of death, but by the futility of their pride in
wishing somehow to overcome it.

The third "poem" is the longest, and more clearly than the
others a version of pastoral elegy. It conforms to the definition
of a funeral celebration of "a dead poet by another of equal
merit." As in *Lycidas* (25–36), one reads a celebration of the
life of the dead, and a deploring of the cruelty of circumstance.
In *Lycidas* that circumstance is the early and seemingly unjust
death of the promising youth (1–14); in Gray it is the circumstances of life itself, of birth, of poverty, but here we find a
realism unknown in the conventional pastoral: an unsentimental
recognition that together with the mute inglorious Miltons there
may also be buried here the Cromwell guiltless of his country's
blood. The expression of grief is also subdued; whereas Milton's
speaker joins his mourning with that of nature itself, Gray's
shows no impulse to mourn for those he has never known.

This *Elegy* consists of two parallel narratives: the first celebrates
the lives and deaths of the anonymous villagers; the second, the
life and death of the anonymous poet whose epitaph concludes
the poem, and is presented as a restrained but honorable memorial for one who is "mindful of th'unhonoured dead." Meditation on these buried lives leads him implicitly to the theme of

his own buried life. Appropriately, he who has sensed that "here may rest . . . some mute inglorious Milton" is not himself mute and, though a poet, is not a Milton. What he shares with the villagers is obscurity imposed by circumstances and a desire to be remembered. The evidence that this anonymous poet is the speaker of the poem himself is complicated, but one aspect of pastoral elegy suggests the first important argument. In an essay on *Lycidas,* Northrop Frye comments that in this genre the poet whose death is mourned is often a kind of "double or shadow" of the elegist.[12] In this poem Gray discreetly conflates the two, mourner and mourned; the imagined body in the imagined grave is not an other like himself, but a projected self, an *achieved* self.

This analysis of the *Elegy* into three "poems" reveals, first, that it is a web of distinct but related themes. Second, it not only makes clear that the poem's mode of organization is associative but also reveals the paths by which the mind of the speaker moves from one theme to another, sometimes returning at a later state to an "argument" which had been deserted earlier. And perhaps more important, it helps to show why some lines or entire stanzas should seem so rich in their apparent simplicity. Since certain elements "belong" equally to different "poems," they became remarkably resonant or multivalent within the whole.

Consider, for example, the first line of stanza 2, "Now fades the glimmering landscape on the sight." Aside from the slightly unexpected shift toward the pastoral which it enacts, it subliminally evokes other themes. I take this stanza to be the first in the second "poem," the meditation on the desire for memorials. The phrase "fades the glimmering landscape" describes the appearance of the sunset, but it also hints at that more universal fading of all worldly things which will later be taken up explicitly, and "glimmering" particularly well evokes the dissipation of material as well as of natural glories. The line's primary or paraphraseable meaning, "Night is coming," anticipates the metaphorical restatement of the theme of the poem, which occurs much later in a pivotal stanza (85–88). And as we shall see, the passivity of one who can do nothing but watch, as the landscape seems to dissipate like dew, establishes a perceptual perspective that will be developed throughout the poem—often at levels other than sensory perception. Many other lines are equally rich when seen as a multicolored veil of references, motifs, and allusions.

Most crucial, however, is a recognition that all three of the "poems" conclude with the epitaph which has been so baffling to many readers. I have already suggested that it conforms, however obliquely, to the conventional ending of the graveyard poem, calming the harried sensibilities of the reader with assurances of divine triumph over death. In relation to the second "poem," it constitutes a suitable memorial, both because it preserves the memory of the dead, and because it serves as a means of communication between the dead and the living; we, Gray's readers, construe it, and within the world of the poem it is also read by that "kindred spirit" who "reads the lay." (This situation is analogous to the conclusion of *Eloisa to Abelard*, where Eloisa finds satisfaction in imagining a similarly attenuated means of clinging to life.)

And finally, as the conclusion of the "elegy" for the anonymous by the anonymous, the rather complicated dramatic situation Gray so quickly sketched in creates for the speaker a future situation parallel to his present one. He who is set apart by his sensitivity and is "mindful" (which suggests empathy as well as mere awareness) of these humble people, is similarly honored by some future stranger who can also "read." (The ability to "read" in the context of this poem is virtually synonymous with acuteness of sensibility.) The tenuous "voice of nature" cries from the tomb and is heard, the universal desire is satisfied. Hence there is a lyric resolution of feeling.

In the preceding analysis, several reasons for regarding Gray's *Elegy* as closely akin to the "greater Romantic Lyric"[13] have been stated or implied: the establishment in the introductory stanzas of an acutely sensitive mind recording the minute particulars, physical and expressive, of the scene before it; the psychological-associative mode of organization throughout the poem; a conclusion that is best understood as the completion of an emotional rather than a narrative or logical pattern. But since the notion of an "impersonal lyric" is, for most readers I suspect, virtually a contradiction in terms, the nature of the evasive speaker of the *Elegy* demands further discussion.

One might say that the *Elegy* is implicitly, rather than explicitly, a lyric. The ordering consciousness, the meditative mind, is notably reticent and unobtrusive. The poem begins as the kind of lyric I have called "pure"—that is, a lyric in the first person in which there is nothing of critical interest to be gained from separating the speaker from the implied poet—or in which we are actually invited to identify the two—as in *Tintern Abbey* or "Frost at Midnight." That the *Elegy* begins in such a mode is indirectly supported by the number of essentially biographical critics who have looked for congruences between Gray and the unknown poet portrayed in these lines. But a curious and unusual transposition occurs during the course of the *Elegy*. What began as a "pure" lyric becomes an "impersonal" lyric of the narrative sort: the first-person reference simply fades away. One might argue that the motive for this disappearance is partly external: allegiance to a poetic decorum which distrusted the private, the particular, or anything that pretended to be either. Whether or not this motive was a conscious one, the transformation is functional thematically—the *Elegy* is concerned with falling darkness, the inevitable obscurity of death. Individual identity eventually disappears, it says, and all that will be left of us is those few lines carved upon the tomb. Even more interesting is that the disappearance is consistent with all that we can infer (and though there are many signs, the reader must depend heavily upon inference) about the psychology of the speaker.

It has long been a cliché to note Gray's debt here to "Il Penseroso." But while verbal echoes and more general analogies with Milton's ambience and setting are assuredly present, a specific comparison between the speakers yields some rather startling disparities. I argued in an earlier chapter that lyric portrays a mind through its perceptions. The things described (and implicitly sought out) by Milton's and Gray's speakers are similar; but their consciousnesses are very different, in one sense opposites. Throughout "Il Penseroso" the speaker actively, even passionately, invokes his goddess Melancholy. Gray's speaker, on the contrary, is passive, never calling but called: "Melancholy mark'd him for her own" (120). And this is an accurate description. The consciousness of Gray's speaker is a transparency, always defining itself indirectly, from the beginning almost wholly displaced into things outside itself. Moreover, those things are themselves made known more by absence than presence, more through negation than assertion. The villagers' lives are almost entirely described, for example, as a series of things that are "no more": "For them no more the blazing hearth shall burn, / Or busy housewife ply her evening care," and so on.

Furthermore, aside from the single personal pronoun of the first stanza, the closest the speaker ever comes to direct self-expression, undisguised confession, is toward the end of the poem in stanza 22 (85–88):

> For who to dumb Forgetfulness a prey,
> This pleasing anxious being e'er resigned,
> Left the warm precincts of the chearful day,
> Nor cast one longing, ling'ring look behind?

This is the only stanza, aside from those of the epitaph, which seems to me to belong to all three "poems"; as well as being a fairly direct lyric utterance, it also comes nearer than any other stanza of the *Elegy* to summarizing the theme of the poem. And, as one might expect, it reveals telling clues as to the sensibility of the speaker.

The paraphraseable content of the stanza is something like this: "Although life is not all pleasure, who has ever given it up without wishing that he need not, without the desire to be remembered?" But in the poem this statement is formulated much less directly. The stanza is cast in the form of a rhetorical question (one which, like the others in the poem, implies a negative answer).[14] It suggests ambivalence toward life itself in the oxymoron "pleasing anxious being"; the now-anonymous speaker imagines himself, and mankind, as passive objects, "prey" not only to "Forgetfulness" but to darkness and death. And the stanza contains two more euphemisms for "die": "resign'd" and "Left the warm precincts of the cheerful day."

This last metaphor, though, like so many others in the poem, verges upon triteness or proverbial familiarity; and yet in this context, it is both appropriate and satisfyingly inevitable, for it reminds us that the action described in the first four stanzas has (like all great poetry) a symbolic as well as a merely descriptive purpose. The opening description of twilight scenery and sounds renders in sensory terms that existential situation which the speaker dreads and yet knows is inevitable: night must fall, night *is* falling. Line 87 deliberately recalls that opening, but now the implicit metaphor is made explicit.

Stanza 22 further characterizes the speaker. Like the entire *Elegy*, it has many present participles, words which indicate process, a sense of things present yet passing. This significant manipulation of grammar (like the description by negation which enables Gray to describe the villagers and the youth in the present or future tenses, creating an impression of life at once concrete and evanescent) is subtly evocative. The lyric consciousness is forever poised helplessly before ineluctable natural processes and can only cast "one longing, lingering look behind." Thus Gray achieves effects similar to those of Keats in "To Autumn"— a paradoxical representation of motion-in-stasis. Another aspect of language also contributes to one's sense of the fragility and transparency entailed by this lyric perspective: throughout the poem everything seems to be moving *away from* the speaker. Day is "parting," the cattle "wind" away, the plowman disappears, the glimmering landscape "fades." Even such "poetic" inversions as "Now fades the glimmering landscape on the sight" are suggestive of the way the speaker perceives his world: he remains precariously fixed before a reality that perpetually dims and recedes. Hence the most unusual manifestation of effacement, the passing away of the "I" into an "other" addressed as "thee," and then described as the buried "Youth to Fortune and to Fame unknown," is an example of grammar (or point of view) responsive to poetic theme. In fact, the entire poem implicitly dramatizes and embodies the various meanings of "passing away," which according to the *OED* has since the Middle Ages been a euphemism for death, but which also means "to elapse," "to depart," "to cease to be," "to relinquish."

Here is yet another reason why the epitaph is a fitting conclusion. Against this background of flux, and when the very selfhood of the speaker has faded away, the epitaph stands out as the one fixed object, however "frail." (Ironically, we are told that for this evanescent soul repose itself is but "tremb'ling hope.") And I want to suggest one further reason for the concluding epitaph, though my rationale is admittedly somewhat more speculative. If one submits Gray's lyric speaker to the kind of psychological analysis that the Romantic lyric speaker usually invites, one discovers a psyche persistently defending itself against in-

tense emotions. The defenses appear in numerous ways: through
the cautious indirections of verbal expression; through rhetorical
questions, descriptions by negation, and describing what is *not*
there; through the limited emotional range the speaker seems
to permit himself, avoiding, as we have seen, the conventional
terrors of the graveyard meditation as well as the ritualized,
hyperbolic expression of grief indigenous to the pastoral elegy.
What we find instead is gentle nostalgia, poignant memories,
and resignation. Hence the poem's avoidance of direct speculation about the speaking self is perfectly consistent with all else
we can infer about his emotional and psychological nature. His
very reticence about himself and his eventual near-obliteration
become—in the light of the various signs I have mentioned—a
way of creating a self-portrait after all.

"Resignation" is a key word for my analysis. It is one of Gray's
many euphemisms for death, but more broadly it indicates an
attitude toward life, the world, and experience that the speaker
displays throughout the poem: his stoic acceptance of the inevitable. It also aptly describes the concluding action of the poem,
as the speaker faces directly, at last, the things that he implicitly
fears: early death, blighted promise, and obscurity. But he faces
them vicariously, by means of the youth whose epitaph he reads.

Gray's original ending, as I noted, consisted of a flat declaration that one should be "resigned" to fate. But if one reads
the present conclusion as an imaginary burial of the self, figured
forth as an "other," one sees that the platitudes of the original
have been translated into a richly evocative "realization." The
speaker has "resigned himself," both in relinquishing the personal pronoun (and all that it suggests) and in disclosing that
the "burial" of the young poet is a burial of all hope of fame.
The vicarious, indirect mode of this solution is completely in
character with all we have seen of his tendency to avoid the
intense or the spontaneous. A modern critic is unavoidably
tempted to read the image of burial as a sign of repression;
certainly speaking often of oneself in the third person may be
a kind of linguistic defensiveness. (One remembers Joyce's neu-
rotic James Duffy in "A Painful Case," who was in the habit of
composing brief narratives about himself in the third person.)
Without committing oneself to a psychoanalytical reading,

however, one still may see that the "burial" makes sense of other elements besides the poem's fictional "characters." Understanding that the "Youth" is an imagined, displaced version of the speaker helps explain the extraordinary density of literary allusions in the lines describing the buried poet (97–116). Critics who have asked whether they aptly describe Gray himself have not, in fact, been thinking in quite the way I have been suggesting here. Such a poet as is described in these lines pointedly lacks the quasi-realistic, natural quality of the poem's other figures; his literariness seems deliberately obtrusive. Here is Milton's "Penseroso" as he might appear to others.[15] And given the speaker's sober reflections, already revealed, about the "rude Forefathers," this "hoary-headed Swain," who seems to belong to the world of Spenser's *Eclogues* or Milton's *Lycidas*, reminds us by his stylized conventionality that he represents a disguised and idealized version of the speaker himself. This passage, more denseiy allusive than anything that preceded (despite the earlier Miltonic echoes), shows itself part of the speaker's "strategy" of self-effacement only, of course, in the context of the various other aspects of that strategy I have been discussing. The subtle but clearly felt unity of this poem, as should be clear by now, will not permit a full apprehension of any part or aspect—even the ostensibly detachable epitaph—in isolation from the whole.

As the remarks of some critics I have already quoted indicate, the temptation has often been to regard the concluding section of the *Elegy*, however impressive in itself, as an excrescence which Gray failed to integrate into the body of the poem. (The critical "Beauty is truth" passage at the end of Keats's "Ode on a Grecian Urn" is a similar example.) But if my analysis of the *Elegy* is correct, then the disappearing "I" and the youth and swain and epitaph which emerge at the conclusion are in fact merely the culmination of a pattern of reticence, indirection, or disguise which the speaker has manifested all along. They are the completion of a process begun in the opening lines, and they constitute a final reminder that this is a lyric, that we are dealing with a carefully individualized (though also universalized) lyric speaker, even though that individuality takes the peculiar form of self-effacement. Finally, by conflating the idea of death, a tombstone with its memorial, and a consolatory tribute by one

who survives, the final stanzas—like the recapitulation of certain
sonata or symphony movements—bring back in one final, grand
synthesis, all the major "themes" (and, in the terms I have been
using, all the major "poems") initially sounded as this work's
distinctive strains even in the opening stanzas.

7

Pastoral into Lyric
The Deserted Village

The speaker of *The Deserted Village* is a penseroso who believes himself a prophet; and it is from this paradox that most problems in reading the poem have arisen. Indeed, he proclaims his "prophetic" themes—the historical issue of enclosure, the universal dangers of luxury and pride. He uses rhetorical and poetic techniques associated with public rather than private modes of discourse (apostrophe, personification, the heroic couplet). Even the more intimate aspects of the poem, such as the speaker's memories of "sweet Auburn," are embodied in the quaint artifices of an already outmoded classical genre, the pastoral. Yet *The Deserted Village* is quite as lyrical as the *Intimations Ode:* in fact, the two share a subject and a theme—the discrepancy between a past and a present world, nostalgia for a paradise lost, the painful but ultimately stoical recognition that you can't go home again. And finally, each is concerned with the importance for poetry of this loss.

To read *The Deserted Village* as fundamentally private and lyrical is, of course, exactly contrary to the usual approach. Goldsmith himself asked us to see it as a political statement, but he was also apparently conscious of a disjunction between his poetic text and the contemporary reality it purported to describe. In the letter of dedication to Sir Joshua Reynolds, Goldsmith writes, "I know you will object (and indeed several of our best and wisest friends concur in the opinion) that the depopulation [the poem] deplores is no where to be seen, and the disorders it laments are only to be found in the poet's imagination." In defense of his theme, Goldsmith adduces his own experience: "I have taken all possible pains, in country excursions, for these four or five years past, to be certain of what I allege; and that all my views and enquiries have led me to believe those miseries real, which I here

attempt to display."[1] This ingenuous remark recalls La Roche-
foucauld's cynical maxim to the effect that travelers invariably
see what they expect to see; but it is congruent with Goldsmith's
perhaps intuitive and spontaneous use of the lyric, and hence
subjective, voice.

Had it not been for the length of *The Deserted Village* (430
lines), readers might have been quick to discount Goldsmith's
own statements about the poem's historical accuracy and to assert
its obvious subjectivity, to read it as a lyric. In terms of my typology of lyric, the poem wavers between the pure personal and
pure rhetorical types. It has a first-person speaker who is but
slightly distinguished from the "implied poet"; but he alternates
between personal expressions and rhetorical adjurations directed to an audience which is both actual ("statesmen") and
figurative ("Luxury," "sweet Poetry"). To period specialists who
have written about the poem, early and late, the unmistakable
lyrical element has apparently been either perplexing or em-
barrassing. In 1785, John Scott criticized the work's illogic:
"Modern Poetry has, in general, one common defect, viz. the
want of proper arrangement. . . . *The Deserted Village* would have
pleased me better, if all the circumstances relative to Auburn the
inhabited, had been grouped in one picture; and all those relative
to Auburn the deserted, in another."[2] The lyrical, associative
order is, for Scott, no order at all.

In the twentieth century, critics have emphasized the biographical and historical contexts of the poem, and its lyricism has
specifically been regarded as problematic. The "intrusion of the
I," as one critic calls it, provokes debate and requires excuses. It
has been explained as a manifestation of "the Tory mind" (embodied in the historical Goldsmith), as a voice of "lyrical simplicity" which is said to have been chosen as a rhetorical device
because it is antithetical to the moral strength toward which the
poem works its conclusion. Tone, perspective, and social commentary together, according to this reading, project "the moral
dimension of the speaker's argument and [appropriate] emotions to fit it." The quasi-lyrical stance is thus itself seen as a kind
of metaphor, a "deliberate technical instrument through which
the poet builds a bridge between the poet and the reader."[3]

Along with this apparent need to see the obtrusive first person
as a subordinate technical device and nothing more, there exists

much confusion concerning the poem as a coherent and organic whole. As with so many of the other works under scrutiny here, readers have puzzled over the apparent disjunction between the conclusion (the speaker's apostrophe to poetry) and the rest of the poem. The issue of historical accuracy has been a constant: whether or not village depopulation was in fact being caused by enclosure. Finally, there has been discussion among readers about the idealization of Auburn's vanished populace, about the somewhat arbitrary declaration of luxury as villain, and about an alleged discrepancy between the subject matter or content and the speaker's response to it: why does Goldsmith (or, more precisely, his speaker—though critics have tended not to make the distinction) feel so intensely about the despoiling of a village that never was, by conditions that did not in fact exist?

The answer, presumably, is that historical and emotional realities do not necessarily coincide, and that *The Deserted Village* is coherent and interesting chiefly as an expression of the latter. If we trust the teller rather than the tale, the poem is seen to have a powerful and sufficient integrity. Perhaps more than any other work discussed in this book, *The Deserted Village* recalls most specifically Milton's technique in "Il Penseroso": the totality of impressions, memories, and responses expressed by the speaker add up to the portrayal of a fully coherent self. *The Deserted Village* is a poem in which "the feeling therein developed gives importance to the action and situation, and not the action and situation to the feeling."[4] And if this speaker is, as I asserted at the beginning, a penseroso unconsciously posing as a prophet, that, too, may be seen as a significant act of self-revelation.

The poem may conveniently be divided into seven stages, each beginning with an apostrophe. The first two are addressed to "Sweet Auburn" (1 and 75); the third to "blest Retirement" (97); the fourth to "Ye friends of truth, ye statesmen" (265); the fifth to "Sweet Auburn" again (337); the sixth to "Luxury" (385); and the last to "Sweet Poetry" (407). In the first two sections (1–224), the speaker observes the ruin that has befallen the village, and then considers its personal significance to himself; he cannot retire here, he finds, and he reminisces about the lost home and friends of his youth. The next section, which is addressed to statesmen (265–336), shows a broadening of perspective and an inducing of causes from effects. We move from description of place to the forces which caused its ruin, from the concrete to the relatively abstract. Having examined the moral and emotional implications of this disturbing displacement of population, the speaker returns to contemplate Auburn once more, noting that its inhabitants are now being driven from the "bare-worn common" to the city. Soon, he imagines, they will have been driven still farther, to the wilds of America, a place he evokes with vividness, if with little geographical accuracy. The penultimate climax (385ff.) marks a new level of abstraction and generality, effecting the personification of Luxury as villain. Finally there is the apostrophe to poetry, his muse (407), who, like the villagers, has fled with the rural virtues. The poet, like the village itself, is deserted at last.

This summary begins to clarify the emotional dynamic of the poem—a continuous movement back and forth between past and present, not only the past and present of personal memory but also of social, political, and moral experience. The speaker meditates upon what the desertion of Auburn means to himself, what it implies about society, and what it tells us about human virtue in general. The vilification of Luxury as the cause of the fall (rather than the associated and more conventional pride) is the most peculiar and also the most individual feature of the poem. As we shall see, however, the choice is appropriate given what we learn about the organizing consciousness.

The emotional springs of the poem are, of course, the speaker's impossibly idealized memories of Auburn as a pastoral golden world. Memory is indeed selective, but the poet's use of idealizing pastoral conventions is in this context most significant. In his description of the lost paradise, Goldsmith's most immediate literary model is, I believe, Pope's *Pastorals,* that sixteen-year-old's wonderfully precocious assimilation of classical, Spenserian, and Miltonic conventions.[5] Auburn, in memory, is a landscape of "brooks" and "plains," of "bowers" and "glades" and "groves"; it is peopled with "nymphs" and "amorous swains," who tend "lowing herds" and "sport" upon the "green."

But the affinities with pastoral are much deeper; for pastoral, wrote Pope, renders "a perfect image of [a] happy time; which, by giving us an esteem for the virtues of a former age, might recommend them to the present." He urges that the pastoral should have a simple "fable," "the manners not too polite nor too rustic; the thoughts are plain, yet admit a little quickness and passion." He declares, however, that the poet ought to choose only pleasant aspects of life for his re-creation of the golden world: "We must . . . use some illusion to render a Pastoral delightful; and this consists in exposing the best side only of a shepherd's life, and in concealing its miseries."⁶ Although Goldsmith pointedly evokes the artifice of pastoral, the strong lyric impulse in the poem makes it unclear whether this one characteristic, the omission of "miseries," is merely conventional or whether it bears witness to the selective nature of memory, that of the poem's controlling consciousness.

Similarly modified is the most familiar of all pastoral conventions—the pathetic fallacy. This device implies an Edenic harmony between man and nature in the pastoral world. It might also be understood as the narrative poet's conventional means of suggesting the phenomenon psychologists now call "projection." In *The Deserted Village* (a pastoral filtered through a lyric consciousness), the device of pathetic fallacy pervades the depiction of the landscape. The speaker perceives human and—significantly in this case—familial qualities in nature; or else their poignant absence is starkly evoked.

Hence the reigning trope of this poem is personification. As the speaker moves back and forth between memory and present reality, a series of contrasting characters emerges, drawn by his imagination out of the past and present landscapes. Beginning with the opening phrase, "Sweet Auburn," the village is rendered as a feminine presence, "loveliest" of her kind, and "smiling." Her most emphasized quality is "charm," a word repeated five times in the opening section.⁷ Auburn is also, implicitly, a mother, the home of the speaker's "youth" (6), and she is now forcibly separated from her "children" (50). After the brief comment, "Ill fares the land, to hastening ills a prey / Where wealth accumulates, and men decay" (51–52) (the first hint of a social theme), the speaker returns to a muted characterization of this rural land as a frugal housewife (58–62) who once "spread her wholesome store, / Just gave what life required, but gave no more." But now, "Sweet Auburn, *parent* of the blissful hour" (my emphasis) is "forlorn" (76), "tangling" (78), "ruined" (78).

In dramatic (or possibly melodramatic) conflict with this tragic mother is a parallel series of male figures. The "tyrant" (37) or "master" (39), in perpetrating enclosure of the land, becomes the "spoiler" (49) of "Sweet Auburn," responsible for her ruin. "Ruin" is a significant word because it has quite different connotations depending on what it describes. Applied to a village, it suggests a physical state ("Sunk are thy bowers, in shapeless ruin all, / And the long grass o'ertops the mouldering wall"— 47–48); in relation, however, to the figurative identity of Auburn as woman and mother, "ruin" suggests the other kind of fall, so often denoted in Goldsmith's time by that word.

That the speaker makes this identification at least subconsciously is manifest in the prominence of the abandoned female figure throughout the poem; she seems to appear every time he needs a simile. The first instance occurs early in the "personal" section, with reference to the watercress gatherer, "yon widowed, solitary thing":

> She, wretched matron, forced in age, for bread,
> To strip the brook with mantling cresses spread,
> To pick her wintry faggot from the thorn,
> To seek her nightly shed, and weep till morn:
> She only left of all the harmless train,
> The sad historian of the pensive plain.   (131–36)

When the poem becomes fixed upon social themes, this figurative identification continues. The speaker, just before mentioning the word "luxury" for the first time, describes nature this way: "While thus the land adorned for pleasure all / In barren splendour feebly waits the fall" (285–86). There immediately follows an aging "fair female" who assumes a meretricious finery and "shines forth, solicitous to bless / In all the glaring impotence of dress" (293–94). And the fate of her children is no better. One of the dangers that awaits them in the city is the usual melodramatically evoked fate. The "poor houseless shiv'ring female" once "wept at tales of innocence distressed"; but now she too is "lost":

> her friends, her virtue fled,
> Near her betrayer's door she lays her head.   (331–32)

To this point I have avoided discussing the two climactic and most problematic personifications—"Luxury" and "Sweet Poetry," which appear in the section of the work primarily concerned with broader moral issues. In keeping with the pattern observed so far, one is male, the other female, and the two are opposed. "Luxury" is the general vice implicit in the actions of "masters," "tyrants," "spoilers." Goldsmith presents Luxury as a conventional seducer, whose "potions, with insidious joy / Diffuse their pleasures only to destroy!" (386–87). Poetry, the "loveliest Maid," is the last and most important in the series of "charming nymphs" endangered by "sensual joys" and "degenerate times of shame" (408–9). She is linked to Auburn, and not only by the epithet "sweet"; like the village, she is the mother of virtue: "Thou guide by which the nobler arts excel, / Thou nurse of every virtue" (415–16). But alone of all the female figures, Poetry is not seduced and ruined by Luxury. In order to escape this fate worse than death, however, she must flee. Hence the conclusion in which the speaker bids his muse farewell: the ruin of his homeland means the loss of his poetry.

This loss (again reminiscent of Wordsworth's *Intimations Ode*) is sorrowful in itself, of course, but the loss seems secondary in the speaker's mind to the ruin of Auburn, which is the intensely painful center of the poem. And although the consistent metaphorical organization I have traced through the poem gives a more ordered account of its structure than have the traditional historical or biographical readings, the psychological impetus of the lyric speaker remains to be explicated. In other words, having followed the figurative "melodrama" of Auburn's ruin within the historical, social, and moral dimensions of the poem, the reader may still wonder why Goldsmith's speaker conceives of his loss in these personified terms, as a conflict between the land and her master, the maid and her seducer, Luxury and Poetry. (Wordsworth, by contrast, images his experience as a plot in which nature, the benevolent foster-mother, adopts the highborn orphan soul and does her best to make it forget "that Imperial palace whence he came," thus effecting a similar loss.)

I remarked earlier that the speaker's consistent personification invests the landscape with human, even familial qualities. Auburn, maternal "parent of the blissful hour," has been ruined, and the speaker, adult and dispossessed, must come to terms with his loss. Aside from the particulars, of course, this situation is by no means unique, but is, in a sense, universal. Nor is my observation that some such loss lies at the heart of the poem entirely new. In a brief but provocative essay called "The Broken Dream of *The Deserted Village*," Morris Golden argues that the poem is fundamentally concerned with "the author's anguished discovery, spurred by events in his own family, that every child must grow up." It is a poem, in short, about innocence and experience, "the contrast between himself as a homeless wanderer and the family security of the past."[8] Even if we ignore the biographical evidence Golden uses (for I am concerned not with Goldsmith himself but with his poetic speaker), this observation remains valid, I think. But I would wish to explore further its particular applications to the speaker and structure of the poem. *The Deserted Village* subtly but unmistakably dramatizes this speaker's obscure, powerful feelings deriving from what Freud would later term "the family romance."

The emotional as well as the metaphorical structure of the poem makes sense if we recognize that "Sweet Auburn" is (figuratively) the speaker's mother, and that he, being one of her children, shows that he has always wished to preserve and affirm the relationship by retiring to her bosom. There is an adolescent boastfulness in his expressed disappointment that he cannot now, as he intended, "Amidst these swains . . . show [his] booklearned skill" and tell of his adventures in the world (90). The universal son's affection for his mother, we recognize, largely accounts for the intensity of his responses when he discovers that the imagined homecoming is impossible.

But a deeper, one can only call it an unconscious, dimension of this attachment is also revealed by the speaker's language. Persistent sexual undertones are heard in his descriptions of Auburn and of the life lived there. Not only are there surprisingly frequent references to innocent lovemaking (14, 29–30, 117, 249–50, 362, 375–78); in addition the speaker frequently refers to the "bowers" of this conventional pastoral world, which once had so much "charm." A bower, the conventional term for a sheltered retreat, is also (as in Spenser's pastoral "Bower of Bliss") a lady's boudoir. Furthermore, Goldsmith's paradise is repeatedly said to be inhabited by "swains." This poetic term was often used in pastoral poetry as a synonym for "rustics," but still much in use in the eighteenth century was the meaning of "a gallant or lover." It is the word Goldsmith's speaker characteristically uses to describe the members of his own generation, sons and lovers. As Golden remarks, the older males (the vicar, school-master, etc.) presumably perceived as the speaker remembers them, are idealized father figures.[9] The word used repeatedly for village activities is "sports"; it is familiar even today, of course, but in a pastoral context it also suggests the earlier sense of "amorous dalliance." A final expression of the speaker's deeper feelings about Auburn occurs in the passage where he describes his fantasies about retirement:

> I still have hopes my latest hours to crown,
> Amidst these humble bowers to lay me down;
> To *husband* out life's taper at the close,
> And keep the flame from wasting by repose.
>
> (85–88, my emphasis)

A poignant source of the speaker's distress and bitterness, it seems, is that he felt himself to be Auburn's mate, as well as her child.

This situation, it will be noted, recapitulates the paradigm of Freud's Oedipus complex. The son, blissfully unconscious of reality, desires perfect union with the mother and intensely despises any rival male—usually the father—who might disrupt the relationship. (The vicar and schoolmaster were too idealized and shadowy to be threatening.) The speaker of *The Deserted Village* finds himself bereft of his mother in a fallen world. We infer from the prevalence of the verb "to flee" in the poem, that his bliss, like Wordsworth's visionary gleam, merely "fled," as bliss is wont to do. He, as much as the village, is "deserted." His apparent strategy for accommodating his grief and rage, which are worked out through the poem, is essentially rationalization: finding emotionally satisfactory reasons to account for his primal loss. He attributes this loss to the intervention of another man, the "master," "tyrant," "spoiler," "Luxury." This "sad historian of the pensive plain" finds satisfaction in angrily denouncing the causes of ruin, in assuming the powerful voice and role of the prophet even as he mourns the loss. And so it is unsurprising if his declarations primarily make private, not public, sense.

This psychosexual dimension of the speaker's responses (implied by his diction, figures of speech, tone) helps to account for his intense revulsion from "Luxury," whom he characterizes, as I have noted, as a seducer. In Goldsmith's language, the older and newer significances of "luxury" were both still in use, according to the *OED*. The older meaning (1340–1812) is "lasciviousness, lust"; Luxuria is one of the seven deadly sins, and this significance therefore belongs to the unconscious personal dynamic of his imagery. The newer meaning (examples cited from 1633 to the present) is the familiar "habitual use of an indulgence in that which is choice or costly, in food, dress, furniture, or appliances," the definition manifestly pertaining to his "prophetic" declaration.

Like Hamlet's language when he is in Gertrude's closet, the speaker's words in this poem reveal his repugnance toward what he registers as the illicit sexual relationship, the seduction of Fair Auburn, by Luxury, "curs'd by Heaven's decree," whom he associates with foulness and corruption. Luxury's potions, says the speaker, lead nations to "sickly greatness," make them "A bloated mass of rank unwieldy woe" (389; 392). This association also accounts for his odd portrayal of that new world into which Auburn's children are exiled, the "horrid shore," or "poisonous fields with rank luxuriance crowned,"

> Where the dark scorpion gathers death around;
> Where at each step the stranger fears to wake
> The rattling terrors of the vengeful snake;
> Where crouching tigers wait their hapless prey.   (352–55)

Here Goldsmith uses "luxuriance" in yet another sense, "growing abundantly, vigorously, lushly." Yet this fertility is cause not for joy but for revulsion, and the vision is obviously colored by the associated meanings of "luxuriance" which fill his mind. The "rankness" of this tropical landscape is affectively linked with the "rank unwieldy woe" that is the result of another kind of luxury. These scorpions, snakes, and crouching tigers therefore connote something akin to rampant libido (the modern reader cannot avoid thinking of Blake's "tyger," and of the luxurious and libidinous dream landscape in Mann's *Death in Venice*).[10] The conclusion of the verse paragraph supports this reading by ending with a virtually gratuitous but telling contrast:

> Far different these from every former scene,
> The cooling brook, the grassy vested green,

> The breezy covert of the warbling grove
> That only sheltered thefts of harmless love. (359–62)

While the imagery involved in this pattern was very likely part of Goldsmith's "rational" design, it is undoubtedly true that dimensions we would call oedipal were not deliberately constructed. Of course, it is paradoxically quite possible for an author unconsciously to create a character who manifests unconscious dimensions; one thinks of Shakespeare first, but many other likely examples can be cited, such as Dickens's Mr. Dombey, who has "only child" rather than "only son" carved on his little boy's tombstone. We cannot know (nor is it important) whether this clear suggestion of complex psychological processes is there by sheer chance or whether we should speak of unconscious revelation, or of design. It seems reasonable, however, to attribute the poem's durable appeal at least partly to the deeply felt authenticity of its speaker's responses—a "truth to nature" which is intuited even by the reader who fails to analyze or articulate it.[11]

The Deserted Village is as paradoxical in poetic technique as it is in theme. Like Eloisa to Abelard, it is entirely Augustan in diction and versification, and also quintessentially lyrical in organization. It is highly conventional in theme and substance, yet startlingly individual in the way the themes are expressed. It is a poem hovering between two worlds, neoclassic and Romantic, and between two versions of pastoral: the old, idealizing conventions of the classical tradition, and the new, "realistic" (later Wordsworthian) version. These two varieties appear, in Goldsmith's poem, roughly to be divided between speaker and subject matter. How he feels (in terms of qualities, and processes displayed) seems generally to foreshadow Romantic conventions; the objects of these feelings belong still to the older world of Colin Clout, of "L'Allegro," of Pope's Pastorals.

Ultimately, The Deserted Village is perhaps best seen as a lament for the ancient form. From the perspective of the speaker, this lament is not only for the village or for rural innocence, but for pastoral poetry itself. A pastoral poet subject to the new historical and literary influences of the late eighteenth century could not write of historical reality as he saw it to be, for that world seemed a calamitous inversion of the bucolic paradise of poetic imaginings. But when he sees "the rural virtues leave the land" and sweet Poetry with them, it is really only the muse of pastoral who departs. In a shift similar to Wordsworth's at the conclusion of the *Intimations Ode*, Goldsmith turns to a poetry concerned with "the rigors of th'inclement clime" (422), which is the world now realized—a world of frequent, cruel suffering. This is a world Wordsworth would also explore. In finding still further ways to evoke and yet redefine the old pastoral ideal, Wordsworth (born the year this poem was published) was to create a very different kind of lyric and pastoral, yet one in many respects already implicit in Goldsmith's poem. Characteristically, the later poet's symbol of natural sorrow, loss, and pain is not a deserted village but a ruined cottage.

8

Tragedy into Lyric
The Ruined Cottage

Wordsworth has never been characterized as a tragic poet because he did not write tragic dramas (except for the early, flawed *Borderers*) and because his vision of man, nature, and human life is consistently affirmative, comic in the broadest sense. Lionel Trilling spoke misleadingly, however, when he referred to Wordsworth's "*incapacity* for tragedy,"[1] for the materials of tragedy are inherent in Wordsworth's great program for poetry, the "intent to weigh / The good and evil of our mortal state." The poet (or rather "bard") must "hear humanity in fields and groves / Pipe solitary anguish." Wordsworth to some degree carried out that program. In one or two of his finest (if not his most typical) poems, tragedy asserts itself unmistakably as a manifestation of that high purpose.

Wordsworth did, apparently, lack the skills of a dramatist. But the essential failure of his most ambitious early work, *The Borderers* (1795–97), cannot be attributed merely to his inexperience as a dramatist or to his youthful immaturity as a poet. He virtually concedes the limitations inherent in this play, with its quintessential Wordsworthian theme of "intellectual murder," when in a long introductory essay he offers psychological analysis of the protagonist and provides other crucial insights which he thereby discloses not to be clearly implicit in the action itself—surely a damning admission. As Richard Sewell remarks in *The Vision of Tragedy*, the Greeks discovered that "only man in action begins to reveal the possibilities of his nature for good, bad, both at once."[2] But for Wordsworth, the focus on tragedy was not upon the human soul in action, but rather upon human suffering in nature. The idea was not his, but he was the first great poet to make it his own. It is a theme, clearly, which defies convincing presentation on a stage, tragic though it may be in spirit. As one character in *The Borderers* observes, "Action is transitory—a step, a blow, . . . Suffering is permanent, obscure and dark, / And shares the nature of infinity."[3]

Drury Lane, not surprisingly, showed no interest in *The Borderers;* but perhaps for Wordsworth the writing of the failed drama had the salutary effect of confirming that his particular tragic theme, like all his best ideas, demanded a lyric perspective. Moreover, he would soon prove that tragic effects need not be restricted to tragic drama. Although tradition will always associate tragedy in our minds with the drama, recent literary history shows many examples of the extension of the tragic effects beyond the stage. Byron's casual gesture toward a poetics (in *Don Juan*), "All tragedies are finished by a death,"[4] has some merit as a working definition. And certainly for tragedy in the Wordsworthian mode death is the last and greatest "evil of our mortal state." When seen in the context of tragedy-as-theodicy (admittedly, the two terms lean toward mutual contradiction), Wordsworth's poetry is shown to be imaginatively peopled with characters we do not hesitate to call tragic, with "natural sorrow, loss or pain" shown as experienced sometimes by himself (or his own quasi-autobiographical surrogate), sometimes by fictional others. Trilling may, of course, have meant only that Wordsworth's poems seldom conclude tragically: their urge toward philosophical reconciliation to mortal loss (the essential note of theodicy) is arguably the overriding purpose of all his best work, including *Tintern Abbey,* the *Intimations Ode,* and *The Prelude.*

To this list I would add the original version of *The Ruined Cottage,* completed in 1799 (MS D).[5] As the last in this series of poems which I read as various experiments with the "greater lyric," the work is interesting not only because it is Wordsworth's effort to reformulate the grounds of tragedy and tragic catharsis in his own terms—within what M. H. Abrams has called "the transaction of mind and nature"—but also because in *The Ruined Cottage* Wordsworth attempts perhaps the most intractable of all the generic innovations we have considered: the shaping of a tragedy (in a structural as well as thematic sense) within the poetic organization of the lyric mode.[6] As in some of the other generic experiments we have considered (*Eloisa to Abelard* or Gray's *Elegy*), the result is unprecedented and powerful.

That Margaret's story is tragic in some sense is hardly contro-
versial. Jonathan Wordsworth writes that

> There seem to be two forms of tragedy—or at
> least two extremes—the fight against odds . . .
> and the tragedy of waste. . . . The first is moving
> because despite human dignity happiness is
> known to be impossible, the second precisely be-
> cause one feels that happiness *was* possible,
> though in fact prevented by circumstance. In a
> curious way *The Ruined Cottage* unites the two.[7]

Still, this valid remark does little to explain the poem's austere,
stark power, nor can I agree with James Averill's argument that
the poem is simply "an investigation into the very sources of his
poetic excitement," an aesthetic experiment with "the pleasures
of tragedy."[8] Furthermore, if we seek explanation by placing *The
Ruined Cottage* in the context of traditional paradigmatic tragedies and traditional poetics of tragedy, convincing answers will
elude us. We might cautiously venture, of course, that Aristotle's
definition of tragedy as "an imitation of an action that is serious
and complete in itself" applies to the story of Margaret, and that
his view of the hero as one "better than we are" is also relevant
in a moral if not a social sense, for Margaret seems to be essentially a saint, or at least an archetypal martyr of love and devotion.
For that reason one cannot really find in her the "error of judgment," the *hamartia,* which contributes significantly to her down-
fall.[9] Wordsworth, however, leaves no doubt about the effect of
her suffering on the sensitive audience; the Aristotelian "catharsis," or something very like it, is here included in the script.
The reader of the poem knows and vicariously participates in
the reactions of both the Pedlar and the first-person speaker. I
shall return later to the most obvious discrepancy from Aristotle,
Wordsworth's denial of the assumption that a tragedy is by definition "directly presented, not narrated." But in any case, to
read the story in the context of Aristotelian theory yields rather
limited results.

Still greater problems emerge in reading the poem as traditionally understood tragedy—philosophical rather than formal
difficulties. If the pure and virtuous Margaret's suffering appears pointless and purposeless (thus pointing the way toward

modern rather than classical premises about life), the witnesses
to that suffering nevertheless experience reconciliation, even a
kind of exultation, in the face of her death and its aftermath;
they do this by means of contemplating the natural order which
has first destroyed and then absorbed her. This response defies
the "logic" even of most earlier tragedies, and it risks bewildering
(if not alienating) the reader. Wordsworth seems to have created
here an ironic, reversed sentimentality: instead of evoking ex-
cessive or unjustified tears in response to a pathetic situation, he
demands joyful acquiescence to a desperately sad story which
seemingly resists acceptance. Unlike Lear or Macbeth, Margaret
does nothing to invite her suffering; her history lacks any apparent reassurances, however small, of moral cause and effect
at work. She is wholly at the mercy of nature, and nature is
merciless. There was little if any precedent for a tragedy so
primitive, so random, so seemingly dependent on blind accident.
(Margaret may be seen, in this regard at least, as an antecedent
of Hardy's Tess or Jude, or even of a few twentieth-century
literary victims.) Like Hardy, Wordsworth avoids suggesting here
purposeful or intelligible divine intervention in human affairs.
He presents only the bleak record of a ruined human life sym-
bolized by a ruined cottage. Nevertheless the Pedlar's and speaker's responses at least suggest those which Aristotle says that
Sophoclean tragedy evokes: the recital of the tale leaves them
"calm of mind, all passion spent."

But to grasp the relationship between the cruel irrationality
of Margaret's fate and the response Wordsworth dramatizes, one
must first recognize that Margaret's tragedy is founded not on
the conflict between character and fate, as in the classical or
Shakespearean tradition, but entirely on the potential suffering
always lurking within man's experience in nature. Perhaps this
formulation sounds existential; however, the salient model for
the kind of tragedy we see in *The Ruined Cottage* is the Book of
Job. Earlier I argued that this book of the Bible provided a
powerful model for the prophetic voice (especially for the prophet
of nature) in eighteenth-century poetry, and I showed how the
concluding speech from the whirlwind inspired much nature
poetry of this era such as *The Seasons*. Biblical scholars tended
to agree, moreover, that Job is a model for tragedy.[10] The book
is resolved by a peculiarly Hebraic version of the deus ex ma-

china, the voice of Jehovah declaiming from the whirlwind the ineffable mystery of the power manifested in his own creation, the machine of the world. Like Margaret's suffering, that of Job is inexplicable in terms of action, of his own earlier deeds, for "there is none like him in the earth, a perfect and upright man, one that feareth God and escheweth evil" (Job 1:18). His sufferings are made intelligible to the reader, however, as the result of a cosmic wager between God and Satan. And in the end all Job's possessions and family are restored (admittedly a puzzling and circuitous reward for good behavior).

The Ruined Cottage is a similar story, but told from a completely human point of view and stripped of its supernatural framework. Like Job's story, the poem has three main parts: the introductory description of the speaker's journey toward the grove, which corresponds to the biblical book's "prologue in Heaven" and implies the theme of natural evil; the story of Margaret as recounted by the Pedlar, which is analogous to the history of Job's trials; and finally, the evocative but precisely rendered vision of the spear grass with "silent raindrops silvered o'er." The Pedlar's response to this vision corresponds to the speech from the whirlwind and Job's consequent recognition of human insignificance in the face of a mysterious, inexorable order.

Much of the Book of Job comprises a debate between Job, his wife, friends, "comforters," and advisors concerning the reason for his sufferings. In *The Ruined Cottage*, this questioning of the ways of Providence (here nature) is present but extremely muted, apparent only in the Pedlar's references to "uneasy" and "restless thoughts," to "foolishness of grief," always dismissed as unworthy, immature responses. Most important, *The Ruined Cottage* is, like the Book of Job, a theodicy, a revelation of the relationship between human suffering and a transcendent order; the apprehension of this relationship, in both works, is shown to be an emotional or imaginative rather than a rational experience. After the speech from the whirlwind, Job says, "I have heard of thee with the hearing of mine ear, but now mine eye seeth thee" (Job 42:5). At the conclusion of Wordsworth's treatment of apparently meaningless human suffering, the Pedlar admonishes the speaker to "no longer read / The forms of things with an unworthy eye." This admonition, he adds, is "wisdom." Thus, despite the realistic texture of the narrative, the work's ancient ancestry underscores Wordsworth's persistent hints throughout the poem that we should not attempt to *understand* Margaret's story (to explain her suffering), but rather, with the speaker our surrogate, to share in it, to experience it so as to find meanings as he does in the essential forms of things and events.

But what does he see, and what *is* it to read with a "worthy eye"? This question returns us to the issue of *The Ruined Cottage* as tragedy. The Book of Job is, in Northrop Frye's terms, a less "displaced" kind of tragedy (displaced, he means, from the mythical) than those Aristotle was describing;[11] despite its prologue and epilogue, the author has yet avoided devices which would overtly elaborate for his audience the fundamental mythos of the tragedy. In the *Anatomy of Criticism*, Frye argues that tragedy reveals in its mythical origins a "mimesis of sacrifice." In the Book of Job, the protagonist is a victim chosen by God precisely because of his goodness, and the audience knows this from the beginning. But our perspective in *The Ruined Cottage* is limited to that of the human characters (and these mainly the observers rather than the sufferer); both this and its "low mimetic" qualities[12] make it ostensibly a more realistic version of a tragic plot. Nevertheless, Wordsworth's preoccupation with human existence in nature and his efforts to strip away all the accretions of society and the language of discursive reason brought him, paradoxically, full circle, back toward the mythic: face to face with those same primal mysteries which many now believe lie at the prehistoric source of tragedy, manifest in the rituals primitive man devised to appease the mysterious powers which he felt controlled his destiny. In *The Ruined Cottage,* Margaret, an eighteenth-century rustic, is yet the most primitive embodiment of tragic protagonist, being simply and essentially the sacrificial victim, a moving example of the Pedlar's truism that "the good die first," one "chosen" only because she happened to live in the path of a deadly train of events.

Although Margaret's story and the lyric speaker's response to it may confuse those who feel comfortable only in a realistic fictional world seemingly ruled by cause and effect (and, ordinarily, partly illuminated by a discursive authorial commentary entirely absent here), the poem when read as a symbolic or mythical tale is both conventional and familiar. If the texture is realistic, and Margaret's story quite "real," "a common tale / By moving accidents uncharactered" (231–32), the plot is just as plainly an archetypal narrative of initiation.[13] As the poem begins, the first-person speaker is journeying across a "wide, bare Common." When he reaches the grove, which contains a shrine and a well, he meets the "wise old man," a wanderer with iron-pointed staff, who sees "Things which you cannot see" (68). This wanderer is a pedlar, and he can feel the awesome, numinous quality of the place, because for him it is a poignant memorial to the dead Margaret. (Perhaps, too, his obvious status as archetypal wise old man hints at his more than usual powers of divination.) After the two men have drunk from Margaret's well, the old man tells the story of a loving woman slowly destroyed by a series of accidents of natural origin—drought, famine, and illness—which lead to her husband's desertion and at last to her own death. The story's concluding words are resonant of myth or parable, as were those of the opening: the two friends go off to seek "A rustic inn, our evening resting place," which (like the conclusion of "The Solitary Reaper") implies that the experience has enlarged the listener's knowledge of life to include the knowledge of death.

The destruction of Margaret is shocking largely because of Wordsworth's use of this radical disjunction between mythical plot and realistic setting. (A similar effect employed for different purposes can be seen in such modern works as Jackson's "The Lottery" or in some of Kafka's tales.) But we must grasp Margaret's role as sacrificial victim, if we are to understand the reactions of the Pedlar and the speaker to her death, which manifest on their part not reason but something akin to the primitive's "participation mystique," as observed by modern anthropologists. The central function of the sacrifice (again according to Frye) is to create a sense of community among the ritual's participants and to reveal something of the nature of the deity, or higher powers. In the most primitive rituals of sacrifice, the body of the victim (often the leader) was ceremonially devoured by the community of participants, hence the feeling of "communion." In *The Ruined Cottage*, as in the Eucharist, this communion is achieved by purely symbolic means. Wordsworth's story, we note, is told at the place where Margaret belonged, and which belonged to her; and each man drinks from what was once her well. But the ritual also suggests that the propitiation of the higher powers, which is from a human perspective the purpose of the sacrifice, means that "in spite of the sense of earthly communion, the body of the sacrificial victim really belongs to another, greater, and potentially wrathful power."[14]

If we pursue this relationship between sacrifice and tragedy, then, we see that the response to ritual sacrifice by the participants is analogous to the audience response to the hero's death in tragedy: a paradoxical blending of the "fearful sense of rightness (the hero must fall) and a pitying sense of wrongness (it is too bad that he falls)."[15] Wordsworth's primary theme in *The Ruined Cottage* is the impersonality, the otherness, of that power, which for him is nature, and its shifting and ambiguous character when seen from the human perspective. The quasi-ritual recounting of Margaret's suffering provides a revelation of man's mysterious bond with nature, which to have is bliss, and to lose is death and hell. (Such are the correspondences of Wordsworthian "natural theology.")

Indications that *The Ruined Cottage* concerns the problem of evil as manifested through man's life in nature are present from the opening lines onward. The narrator first appears in a natural setting alive with an iconographic significance, and fraught with hints of the physical suffering nature can inflict. It is wearingly hot; the sun "feebly glared / Through a pale steam." The sky is hung with "deep embattled clouds." The description suggests various manifestations of "natural evil": the narrator's "toil[ing]" across the "Common" hints that he is an Everyman (like Spenser's knight "pricking on the plaine"). He steps on "bursting gorse"; his feet are "languid," and the "slippery" ground "baffles" them. Nor can his "Weak arm disperse / The insect host which gathered round [his] face." This is no wasteland he travels over (he can imagine the pleasant possibilities of shade and coolness), yet these irritations foreshadow the much greater sufferings of Margaret and prefigure the final epiphany. This is our "prologue on earth"; the stage for Wordsworth's lyrical tragic drama is set.

When the speaker reaches the grove and sees the ruined cottage, Margaret's story told by the Pedlar concretely illustrates the ominous potentialities within the introductory description of nature. Despite the literalness of the story, however, it finally makes little sense as a realistic fiction. To ask why Margaret cannot recover from the loss of Robert, is as futile as to explain in realistic psychological terms why Bluebeard gives his wife the key to the forbidden chamber, or why only one fruit is forbidden in the Garden of Eden. But as a symbolic tale, the tragedy has its haunting and lucid theme: it illustrates the effects of severed natural bonds, and it implies that only man can will their severance.

Margaret's trials begin with the famine and drought. Like Job, however, she and Robert refuse to despair. But then Robert is stricken with a fever (disease was the last of Job's afflictions), and he breaks. He cannot endure, and deserts Margaret to bind himself to another spouse, the army. The money he leaves suggests at once Judas's silver of betrayal and the fee left for a prostitute to find when she awakens alone in the morning. We cannot deny that in Margaret trauma plausibly enough arises from her husband's betrayal, yet the effects which constitute the rest of the narrative seem out of proportion to their causes; such disproportion further reminds us that this is a symbolic structure. The broken marriage symbolizes the dissolution of that primal universal bond with which Wordsworth was everywhere concerned, the marriage of mind and nature. (As Professor Abrams argues, the invariable marriage metaphor in Wordsworth and the other Romantics reveals their appropriation of a biblical strain of imagery. In this instance the marriage is at once literal and symbolic.)[16] When Margaret's marriage ends in desertion, her subsequent history can only display the gradual dissolution of all other remaining bonds. Her elder child is apprenticed (bonded to another, surrogate parent), her younger child dies, and all the while her most immediate relationship to nature, manifested in her garden and cottage, gradually disintegrates. All that remains of a once happy union is the dilapidated cottage, the ruined garden, and "the useless fragment of a wooden bowl."

In establishing that the story of Margaret is akin to the archetypal "mimesis of sacrifice" implicit in all tragedies, and that the Pedlar and lyric speaker respond to the pattern of events in the way prescribed by Aristotle and other theorists of tragedy, I have not yet discussed Wordsworth's techniques of generic appropriation. In *The Ruined Cottage* Wordsworth not only incorporates a tragic plot into a lyric; he also uses specific dramaturgical devices without compromising his essentially lyric perspective. These enable him to emphasize through dramatized action a dimension of tragedy that is, in the drama proper, only implicit: its effect on the audience.

I have suggested that the prologue, the speaker's journey across the "wide, bare Common," implies, with its strong evocations of myth, that "all the world's a stage." When he reaches the grove and hears the story of Margaret, the tragedy proper begins, and the epilogue reveals the Pedlar's and the narrator's response to it. Of course any number of correspondences between Wordsworth's plot, theme, and revealed audience-response, and their analogues in tragic drama, do not answer the literalist's objection that tragedy is action on a stage. *The Ruined Cottage* is not a play in that sense; neither is it Romantic "closet drama." But as I argued earlier, the presence of the "Palmer's Sonnet" does not make *Romeo and Juliet* a lyric poem, nor does the detached omniscient narrator of Meredith's "Lucifer in Starlight" or of Tennyson's "Mariana" make them short stories; similarly, a narrative plot redolent of tragedy does not in itself so categorize Wordsworth's poem. Nevertheless, such partial assimilation by one mode of the generic conventions of another—as this entire study repeatedly demonstrates—results in a new kind of work with unique effects upon the reader.

In specifying the kind of generic assimilation shown in *The Ruined Cottage,* I would observe that it is a complex structure containing a triad of "concentric" personae (to use a term applicable in different ways to both drama and lyric). The reader hears the story of Margaret third-hand, filtered through the consciousness of two others. (Wordsworth's technique here in mediating the painful and difficult story of Margaret looks forward to *Wuthering Heights,* another Romantic work that carefully frustrates our generic expectations.) The narrative core of the poem, however, Margaret's history, is presented in a way more nearly dramatic (if not at all theatrical) than narrative or lyric. This adaptation serves to mediate the primitive tragic theme, and to permit its eventual transmutation into a typically Wordsworthian consolation.

At the same time, the fact that Wordsworth has chosen to distance his protagonist from the reader, excluding direct glimpses into her consciousness and, instead, making her an object of sympathetic contemplation for two observers (and, through them, for us) underscores the work's status as a lyric. However intently the reader may, for a time, focus his attention upon Margaret and her story, still the first, final, and paramount interest is in the reverberations of that story in the minds of two others. They provide not merely the narrative frame but the poem's final significance and its organizing purpose. To repeat Wordsworth's remark from the *Preface* to the *Lyrical Ballads,* "the actions take their importance from the feelings, not the feelings from the action." (One might observe, too, when comparing this tragic poem with the Book of Job, that Wordsworth's shift from a pure narrative into a lyrical mode is implicit in his transferal of the final reconciliation from the tragic protagonist to a narrator-observer and a poetic speaker.) The result is a lyric, though one displaced toward both the dramatic and narrative modes.

The Pedlar tells us Margaret's story in five "acts." The first of these is his exposition (120–85) of how Margaret and her husband, faithful and industrious, lived happily together with their two children. Then the complications begin, with a series of natural disasters: "Two blighting seasons," "a plague of war," economic depression. The couple cheerfully endures until Robert's sudden and wasting disease leaves him weak and embittered. The remaining four "acts" are vignettes of Margaret's progressive decay, observed by the Pedlar as he returns from time to time. The long absences between visits make the progress of her decline more "dramatically" evident, while at the same time emphasizing them as successive views in a lyric perspective. In "Act II" (245–88) Robert has deserted her, and she is struggling to maintain the place; as the Pedlar leaves, she is "busy with her garden tools." But in "Act III" when he returns again, there are surer signs of disintegration (298–360). When he arrives she is absent, out wandering across the fields, and as he waits he hears the lonely infant crying in the cottage. At last Margaret returns and affirms that the signs of physical decline evident in the garden are paralleled by the loosening of her human ties; her older child has been apprenticed, and the baby is clearly suffering from neglect. When the Pedlar next returns ("Act IV") decay and decline are still more pervasive, the garden and cottage being not only neglected but "comfortless" (392–434). Margaret declares that "for her Babe, / And for her little friendless Boy . . . she had no wish to live" (428–29). At the final meeting (434–45), she tells the Pedlar that her final human tie is no more, her baby is dead. The Pedlar leaves, never to see her again. She lingers on until the final bond with nature, life itself, is broken, and she dies.

Considered in the context of drama, the Pedlar plays the role of chorus, commenting on the action as well as reporting it. He describes how Margaret looked and acted, and occasionally quotes her infrequent words. This manner of telling conforms to the classical decorum demanding that violent acts and miserable spectacles occur offstage, to be reported by someone who has witnessed them. It also recalls the Shakespearean practice of having a witness describe unstageable events such as Cleopatra's progress down the Nile or the drowning of Ophelia. The death of Margaret is in fact far less adaptable to the stage than Ophelia's drowning, for it is a slow and prolonged process, and it is inseparable from the congruent changes in the garden and the cottage. The Pedlar is a strange witness; he hovers between chorus and magus, one who virtually brings Margaret back to life before our eyes. (The resurrection is most nearly implied when the speaker, our witness to the Pedlar's reports, "review[s] the woman's sufferings"). Although these two characters are present on the "stage" where the drama has taken place, this technique makes Margaret at once more human and more mysteriously an "other." This is a peculiarly Wordsworthian mystery play.

Wordsworth's overarching lyric purpose requires that Margaret's story be told in the way that it is—moving yet distanced—and for its sake a great portion of the narrative veers toward descriptions of her garden and cottage. The breaking of natural bonds can be illustrated only in this way: they are not mere symbols, but paradoxically literal, concrete embodiments of the theme. (One might note in passing that *The Ruined Cottage* is a far better title than "The Story of Margaret" would have been, for the cottage, as primary symbol, points directly to the theme: as a human artifact made of natural materials its ruin both constitutes and symbolizes the breaking of the bond.) The decay of the garden is not simply an objective correlative for Margaret's spiritual state, as is the deserted grange in Tennyson's "Mariana," for example. There are of course ordinary causal explanations for its decline; weeds do spring up in uncultivated gardens. But it is crucial that we know Margaret partly *through* the garden and cottage, which are her remains and her memorial. We thus associate her with such mythical nature-deities as Demeter. Margaret's increasing irresponsibility as a mother is parallel to Mother Nature's uncaring treatment of her. The simultaneous disintegration of the garden and of the living being illustrates the mystery which the Pedlar seeks to reveal.

Wordsworth also consistently though unobtrusively links Margaret's garden with Eden, and this strengthens our sense of the sacredness of that bond. Frye remarks that the story of Eden is the archetypal tragedy of the Judeo-Christian tradition[17] (one which is, of course, presupposed by the Book of Job); and the Pedlar's descriptions of Margaret's garden and cottage recall that primal loss. In the beginning the happy, loving Margaret lived in a paradisal world where all bonds, familial and natural, held strong; this happiness was "a simple produce of the common day." From her cottage and garden, a *locus amoenus*, radiated other ties. She always gave the Pedlar "a daughter's welcome"; "no one came / But he was welcome," "no one went away / But that it seemed she loved him" (101–3).

The fall of Adam and Eve is a tragedy of actions, "a step, a blow"; for they choose to act, and do so. But after the fall in *The Ruined Cottage* (Robert's illness occurs in autumn), Margaret's only action is to cling to her fraying bonds, loyally if ineffectually. Like Eve in *Paradise Lost* she weeps, but for a loss that is only gradually accomplished, gradually realized. She tells the Pedlar, "I have slept / Weeping, and weeping I have waked." Unlike Eve, she remains in her "broken arbor" (no longer an *arbor vitae*). At first, the garden reflects an undisciplined extravagance, as uncontrolled as Margaret's tears. Its growth parodies that of a healthy and flourishing life—of one human being with another, or with nature. "Worthless stonecrop," "unprofitable bindweed" start up; with "unwieldy wreaths" they "dragged the rose . . . And bent it to earth." "The honeysuckle crowded round the door, / And from the wall hung down in heavier tufts." (Symbolically, the flower seems both to mourn and to warn.) In Margaret's garden, even the apple tree dies (419–26). The final stages of the fall are accomplished after her death, however, when the garden is invaded by those passersby whom the gooseberries and currants "hanging from their leafless stems / In scanty string, had tempted to o'erleap / The broken wall." (An echo sounds here of *Paradise Lost,* IV, 583; perhaps, too, "to o'erleap / The broken wall" is, figuratively, to perform the imaginative act of reconciliation to suffering and loss with which the poem will conclude.) At last the place is invaded by "weeds and rank spear grass, . . . where nettles rot and adders sun themselves."[18]

If Margaret's destruction reveals the mysterious ramifications of that bond between man and nature, then the corollary and antidote to this Wordsworthian tragedy, the effect on the Pedlar's audience, is an appropriate catharsis: the creation and strengthening of new bonds through knowledge of that tragic experience. After showing that for him the "pathetic fallacy" of the elegiac poets figures forth true wisdom concerning man and nature, the Pedlar continues:

> Sympathies there are
> More tranquil, yet perhaps of kindred birth,
> That steal upon the meditative mind
> And grow with thought.   (79–82)

Tragic disruptions like Margaret's may have the power to forge durable sympathies among those left behind, just as the violent death of one person (actual or symbolic) in the ritual of sacrifice strengthens the communal sense of the celebrants, who remain. This is why the Pedlar says that in tales of suffering endurance, paradoxically, resides "a power to virtue friendly."

Variously throughout the poem but particularly at the conclusion, the restoration, strengthening, or new creation of sympathetic bonds between man and nature, man and man, and within man himself, are revealed. Near the beginning, the Pedlar, already initiated into the mystery, says, "Beside yon spring I stood, / And eyed its waters till we seemed to feel / One sadness, they and I" (82–84).[19] After hearing the tale, the speaker declares that Margaret's story "seemed / To comfort me while with a brother's love / I blessed her in the impotence of grief." And as the poem ends, the two men—teacher and student, priest and initiate, friend and friend—go off together toward "their evening resting place," which suggests the traditional conclusion of life's journey, as well as of many smaller ones.

Most important, however, is the fostering of that internal, psychological power necessary for the sustenance of all human bonds, the imagination. The climax of *The Ruined Cottage* is the Pedlar's

vision which, though presented near the end of the work, is
prior both chronologically and psychologically to his association
with the narrator. Returning to this place after Margaret's death,
he says:

> I well remember that those very plumes,
> Those weeds, and the high spear grass on that wall,
> By mist and silent raindrops silvered o'er,
> As once I passed, did to my mind convey
> So still an image of tranquility,
> So calm and still, and looked so beautiful
> Amid the uneasy thought which filled my mind,
> That what we feel of sorrow and despair
> From ruin and from change, and all the grief
> The passing shews of being leave behind,
> Appeared an idle dream that could not live
> Where meditation was. I turned away,
> And walked along my road in happiness.   (513–25)

Frye writes that "Whether the context is Greek, Christian, or
undefined, tragedy seems to lead up to an epiphany of law."[20]
This insight can be directly related to Margaret's mythic role as
sacrificial victim. Even as her suffering and death reveals not so
much a wrathful deity as the mysterious power of impersonal
nature, to which she now entirely belongs ("she sleeps in the
calm earth"), so her endurance, her stoic loyalty to the place
sacred to the memory of the ties which once sustained her, are
for the Pedlar and his listener an emblem of transcendent permanence beyond the "passing shews of being."[21] Tacitly the Pedlar perceives this as he sees the spear grass, symbol of martyrdom,
transformed "by mist and silent raindrops silvered o'er."

In contrast to God's speech from the whirlwind, this epiphany
is remarkably understated, yet it serves the same purpose. One
recalls Job's response, "now mine eye seeth thee." The Pedlar too
has seen, and understood, and can now serve as mediator of this
truth to the younger witness. Yet the Pedlar's vision is not, like Job's,
a direct revelation by the supernatural but rather one deeply felt
by a mind long prepared to receive it in a life spent in pilgrimage
through the natural world (a pilgrimage of one who, as Wordsworth would put it elsewhere, "hath kept watch o'er man's mortality"). The Pedlar is one of those who have learned "to rightly

spell / Of every herb that sips the dew / And every star the heaven doth shew." And this "old experience" has led him, like Milton's Penseroso, to "something like prophetic strain."

This early version of Margaret's story thus embodies a radical natural supernaturalism; it would have shocked Milton, perhaps, even as he might have recognized in the Pedlar a mature embodiment of his own Penseroso. *The Ruined Cottage* is, ultimately, about this process of maturation, about how the meditative man becomes the prophet. For as I argued at the beginning, this is above all a tale of initiation; it is also a lyric poem, chiefly because the initiation belongs to an organizing consciousness separate from, and enveloping, the narrative protagonist. It is best characterized as "lyric tragedy" because it is not Margaret's story but, finally, the unnamed speaker's. It dramatizes the process of his moral-imaginative education in introducing him to the greatest among the mysterious evils of our mortal state: "the good die first / And those whose hearts are dry as summer's dust / Burn to the socket."

In this light, one can understand more clearly the motives for the revisions Wordsworth made when he incorporated this early manuscript into Book I of *The Excursion*. He indicated in a note that the Pedlar (who became "The Wanderer") "is chiefly an idea of what I fancied my own character might have become under the circumstances."[22] In revising he added, mainly, a history of the Pedlar's education and growth, no doubt to lend further credibility to the old man's climactic vision. Wordsworth also both softened the tale of Margaret's suffering and added various allusions to Christianity. These changes are, in light of the archetypal perspective of my analysis, simply a redundant doubling of the theme, for Christ, like Margaret, was an innocent victim whose sacrificial death served to create a communion among those left behind, and to propitiate a deity. From his suffering, too, sprang a paradoxical comfort for those who had witnessed his life and death. (On the other hand, the new Christian framework might be taken to imply the heroine's being merely transposed to a life everlasting—a suggestion pointedly absent from the original version.)

In *The Ruined Cottage*, Wordsworth strains the lyric mode to its limits. We have seen why a new tragic perspective was suited to his treatment of this most philosophically difficult of themes;

the lyricism, besides being the poet's unvarying preference (and, by this time, that of his age) was equally necessary to show how the tragic suffering of one might constitute the moral education of others. The unobtrusive speaker, whose presence creates a double lyric perspective, presumably functions much as do the younger, silent listeners to whom the speaker turns at the end of such lyrics as *Tintern Abbey* or "Frost at Midnight"—poems with notable but far less developed dramatic and narrative components. In these works, too, a speaker's attained natural wisdom, when finally seen as the potential experience of a younger person (identifiable with Dorothy or Hartley), seems to promise its own continuing validity for both, as well as for others. At the same time that he was writing *The Ruined Cottage*, however, Wordsworth was beginning *The Prelude* which, daringly expanding his lyric practice to an unprecedented epic scale, abandons self-proclaimed fictions. Now he would through his own history (or at least a modified, poetically heightened version of it) reveal just how the penseroso had become a "prophet of nature"; and he wrote the *Intimations Ode,* a lyric which internally records the strains of achieving prophetic strain.

9

Wordsworth's *Intimations Ode*
The Fortunate Fall

Of all the poems I have discussed, only Wordsworth's *Ode: Intimations of Immortality from Recollections of Early Childhood* overtly announces itself as a "greater lyric." We can well imagine how peculiar and surprising it must have seemed to its earliest readers. To be sure, the ode was a fashionable form, but no other eighteenth-century example known to me is so frankly private and personal. Accustomed as we now are to such later instances as Keats's "Ode to a Nightingale" or Stevens's ode-like (though not so labeled) "Sunday Morning," we need for the moment to erase our acute consciousness of that Romantic and post-Romantic line of development if we are to recapture anything like the impression Wordsworth's poem must have created. It has affinities, of course, with some of the odes of his immediate predecessors; in both manner and substance it may be interestingly if superficially compared to Gray's "Ode on a Distant Prospect of Eton College." But Gray's exercise in the genre is by comparison highly conventional and public, as the ode was expected to be.

  And so, seen against the background of then current practice, the most salient thing about Wordsworth's effort is the bold new way in which he seeks to reconcile opposites: in order to resolve urgent questions about a personal (perhaps even idiosyncratic) feeling of loss,[1] he proposes a myth redolent of universal human experience. And in order to justify and give authority to the somewhat paradoxical resolution at which he arrives, he invokes—as did some of the other poets we have considered—a Miltonic model: in this case, as I shall argue, no less than the whole of *Paradise Lost*. The *Ode* is full of buried allusions to Milton's epic which indicate a consistent analogue of situation and a congruent pattern of psychological response, that response being to a loss which touches the poem's speaker both as man and as poet. Thus from the perspective of the tradition I have been exploring, Wordsworth's *Ode* is an appropriate conclusion; for it enacts within itself an individual poet's gradual attainment to something like prophetic strain.[2]

A primary theme of the *Intimations Ode* is the transition from innocence to experience, the process of growing up, as Trilling writes.[3] The *Ode* is ostensibly a natural history. But its structure specifically echoes Milton's epic retelling of the Christian myth—a tragedy ultimately less tragic when seen as a step toward higher things. The foremost indication of this parallel is Wordsworth's paradoxical thanksgiving for loss and suffering, for "fallings, vanishings," which he declares after the shift in mood between stanzas 8 and 9.[4] His gratitude is even less equivocal than Adam's, who said, "Full of doubt I stand / Whether I should repent me now of sin . . . / . . . or rejoice / Much more, that much more good thereof shall spring" (*P.L.*, XII, 473–76).

Once heard, this echo suggests the possibility of further parallels between the situation of Adam and that of Wordsworth's speaker. And indeed there are several, though in a characteristic Wordsworthian compression of psychological insight and religious metaphor, the whole experience is transposed into the microcosm of mind and nature. In the *Ode* the mind's "high instincts" assume the role of God the Father; Wordworth's "mortal nature" behaves like Adam and Eve after the Fall, who, conscious of sin, trembled before God as guilty things surprised. When Eve fell, "earth felt the wound" of sin (*P.L.*, IX, 782); in the experience of Wordsworth's speaker, the change is felt as a decay of his own faculties, not of nature. The sign of Adam's innocence was a garden, which, once damaged, all his tilling could never restore. Wordsworthian innocence was manifested in spontaneous imaginative vision, which, once lost, "we are toiling all our lives to find" (116).

According to the *Ode*, the child dwells in an Edenic state ("heaven lies about us . . .") of supreme imagination. But this state, though blissful, is as limited as Eden was. Though "Blessed" in his "heaven-born freedom," the child is also, paradoxically, a prisoner: over him "Immortality / Broods like the day, a Master o'er a Slave / A presence which is not to be put by" (118–20). A slave is still bound, even though his master be divine. And it is one aspect of this particular slave's servitude that he is unaware of his bondage, blinded by his vision. Eden was a walled garden, a symbol of the insight—more explicit in Wordsworth—that ignorance *is* bliss.

In contrast to Adam's fall, the child's is not consciously chosen, nor is it an isolated event. Each story, however, includes an element of seduction. Nature, the kindly nurse and foster mother, innocently offers fruit which, far from being forbidden, is necessary food. Yet this fruit is as dangerous as the serpent's, for it also comes from the tree of knowledge, the fatal apple of worldly experience. But this "naturalization" of the soul is the result of collaboration. Some of the child's own best spiritual qualities, his yearning to know and to be, lead him forward along the inevitable path as he imitates the fallen (adult) state of his parents. Thus he takes what nature offers and gradually leaves Eden; the celestial light fades "into the light of common day."

Adam had an angel to instruct him in the significance of his fall; Wordsworth has a child who is in part an externalized, objectified version of his remembered earlier self, and at the same time a figure of mythic overtones, recalling the holy, archetypal child who is the son of a sky father and an earth mother, and thus a symbol of creative union between spirit and matter. In *Paradise Lost* the Archangel Michael permits Adam a vision of human history which is the last stage of his preparation to depart from Eden. After observing this world to come, Adam exclaims:

> How soon hath thy prediction Seer blest,
> Measur'd this transient World the Race of time,
> Till time stand fixt: beyond is all abyss,
> Eternity, whose end no eye can reach.
> Greatly instructed I shall hence depart
> Greatly in peace of thought. . . .   (XII, 553–58)

In the *Ode* it is the speaker's *own* eye "which hath kept watch o'er man's mortality." But his encounter with his childhood self, the "Mighty Prophet, seer Blest," is as crucial as was Michael's revelation to Adam. The deepest sorrow springs from the knowledge that this child, every child, must lose his original brightness; yet the subsequent climactic and paradoxical joy springs from the same revelation.

Like all profoundly religious insights, this one is a recognition of order, of unity, of community. All is One: the child's "celestial light" and the man's memory of "what was so fugitive." Thus the man may now, through memory, travel back to the edge of "immortal sea." The child is a prophet in Wordsworth's eyes because he looks forward to the man's supreme moment of recognition. And this attribution of prophecy before the nadir of despair in the poem is a silent preparation for the final "access of joy."

Like the divine goodness which makes a fortunate fall of Adam's sin, the enduring and restorative capacities of mind preside over Wordsworth's recognition of gain through loss. The history recounted in the *Ode*, therefore, summarizes and recapitulates an idea familiar elsewhere in Wordsworth, particularly in *The Prelude*, where he describes the "spots of time." These remembered experiences reassert the dominion of mind and have a "fructifying," "vivifying," "renovating" virtue. Through such memories, writes Wordsworth, the mind is "nourished and invisibly repaired":

> A virtue, by which pleasure is enhanced,
> That penetrates, enables us to mount,
> When high, more high, and lifts us up when fallen.
> (*The Prelude*, XII, 216–18)[5]

The *Ode* presents the archetype (in a precise sense) of such experiences, for the history it records is treated as collective and universal, at once individual and shared by all. The phrase from *The Prelude*, "lifts us up when fallen," so relevant to my reading of the *Ode*, hints that the Wordsworthian and universally human fall is, unlike Adam's, a recurrent failure of spirit from which one may repeatedly recover.

The speaker describes sources of strength new to him in maturity; all of them indicate new power and boundaries overcome. All demonstrate the two most essential Wordsworthian values: the dominance of mind over "outward sense" and the ability to hear the still, sad music of humanity. All are born of the marriage of mind and nature. "The soothing thoughts that spring / Out of human suffering" evoke the notion of tragic catharsis, which may be seen as an aesthetic counterpart of the fortunate fall— and in the *Ode* as Wordsworth's translation of Adam's observation

that evil may be turned into good (*P.L.*, XII, 471). The philosophic mind, the supreme Wordsworthian reward, has, unlike
the child's mind, the capacity to grow and to change, to accommodate external realities. It does not imitate, but instead shapes.
Implicit in the *Ode,* then, is *The Prelude*'s declared theme, the
growth of the poet's mind.

I have refrained until now from discussing the most obvious
Miltonic allusion in the *Ode:* from the beginning, the speaker
describes his loss as the disappearance of a "celestial light." This
is Milton's phrase, appearing in the Invocation to Book III, where
the poet mourns his blindness:

> . . . cloud . . . and ever-during dark
> Surrounds me, from the cheerful ways of men
> Cut off, and for the Book of knowledge fair
> Presented with a Universal blanc.   (45–48)

From Milton, too, a visionary gleam was fled, but his solution is
clear and immediate: "So much the rather thou Celestial Light
/ Shine inward, and the mind through all her powers / Irra-
diate . . ." (51–53). Wordsworth's appropriation of the Miltonic
words is characteristic, and invites the reader to explore the
analogy so unobtrusively proposed.[6]

The spiritual loss of vision sustained by Wordsworth's speaker,
figuratively expressed, echoes Milton's references to his own
physical loss. Each knows that nature continues in her course,
that the change is a personal deficiency. Each turns inward in
an attempt to find a new illumination which will enable him to
"see and tell / Of things invisible to mortal sight" (*P.L.*, III, 54–
55). The "Celestial Light" to which Milton turns is the heavenly
muse; Wordsworth's light is childhood's imaginative experience
which he comes to recognize as yet alive, though transformed,
"fallen" into another mode of being.

The "Celestial Light" in its new Wordsworthian context becomes broader in meaning, and a way of wedding particular
with universal experience in the *Ode.* In its various manifestations
as star, ember, and sunset light, it is a metaphor for all human
spiritual experience and development. But its prior, Miltonic
sense of divine poetic inspiration remains relevant to Wordsworth the poet, since the allusion reminds us that Wordsworth's
loss of the gleam had the same poetic implications that troubled

Milton. Thus we recognize a final way in which Milton's theme of the fortunate fall illuminates the *Ode*.[7]

Milton appropriated the epic tradition to convey his myth of the loss of Eden. It is fitting that Wordsworth's psychological version of the same plot is presented in a lyric form. If we wished to describe the poem's generic affinities precisely, we should say that an elegy is resolved by—and into—an ode. This generic transformation subtly dramatizes the notion of the fortunate fall in a guise especially reassuring to the poet, who mourns the loss of "Celestial Light."

Any traditional genre, by virtue of the fact that it *is* traditional, implies its own context. Reading an elegy, for instance, one not only remembers elegiac conventions and earlier examples, one also expects a certain range of themes, attitudes, strategies, styles. The choice of genre is one means of controlling a reader's expectations. In terms of genre, however, something rather curious happens in the *Ode* which critics have not fully acknowledged: the substitution of a major for a minor lyric kind. If one is justified in seeing genres as a significant dimension of the work's meaning, then this shift may itself reflect, at a literary level, the emotional and phenomenological change it describes.

If we attend to the conventional signals, the *Intimations Ode* begins as a pastoral elegy. Bloom is quite correct in noting Wordsworth's debt to *Lycidas* in the first four stanzas where a first-person-singular voice speaks of "something that is gone." In a springtime pastoral world of lambs and shepherds, this voice stresses isolation and loss. In an ironic compression of the elegiac convention in which the speaker typically observes nature herself mourning, Wordsworth's speaker acknowledges that nature's reflection of this loss springs from within: the rainbow, rose, and moonlight are still lovely—only their glory is departed. Yet this elegiac strain abruptly ceases after the speaker poses his overwhelming question: "Whither is fled the visionary gleam? / Where is it now, the glory and the dream?"

The first-person singular is then replaced by a first-person plural, a more public voice which speaks of "our birth," "our life's star." The "I" does not return until after another, even more abrupt change—the modulation from sorrow to joy between stanzas 8 and 9. This middle portion we may call the "ode" proper, for it follows the eighteenth-century convention that the ode should express themes of high import and public character. Odes, declared Plato, should sing the praises of gods and heroes. In the enthusiasm for "Pindaricks" many eighteenth-century critics echoed this exalted sense of the genre's proper sphere; typical among them was John Dennis, who in 1704 wrote that the "greater lyrick," or ode, was the form most suited to the expression of religious truth.[8] The ode was generally ranked near the top of the generic hierarchy and as near epic and tragedy as any lyric could be. Elegy remained near the bottom of the scale. The elegiac voice, therefore, is implicitly the voice of a bereaved shepherd, mourning the loss of his beloved, while the speaker of the ode is ideally a bard, the quintessentially reliable narrator, who "present, past, and future sees."

Assuming that this modulation of a lesser into a greater lyric form is artistically significant, what are its implications? First, one recognizes that Wordsworth has not merely treated Milton's epic theme in lyric form but also that this form has imposed upon him the necessity of treating the theme from exactly the opposite perspective. Milton's treatment of the universal human experience of loss ("the root of all our woe") begins with a symbol, the prototypical man, Adam. Milton's strategy is to "humanize" the actors of this drama—his various abstract representatives of man, woman, good, evil. His challenge is to make them into credible human characters with the power to evoke empathy from readers. When, less than two centuries later, Wordsworth attempts the same theme, however, it is apparently impossible to write an epic based on mythical material, as he reveals in describing his search for a theme in Book I of *The Prelude*. The epistemological revolution, the rise of empiricism manifest in the Romantic ethos, now finds most convincing a truth that is grounded in human experience rather than one that is the testimony of divine revelation.

Thus for Wordsworth (as for most of the Romantics) the lyric had a special appropriateness and a special validity, being the mode which most readily supports the portrayal of unique and private experience. This subjective angle of vision, however, always threatens to imply solipsism: how can the poet be sure that what seems true from his perspective is true from that of others? Wordsworth's solution is evident in the *Ode:* instead of beginning with revealed truth, as Milton did, he is constrained to begin with his own lived truth, but he knows he must still bridge the gulf between himself and other men.

He does so by means of this generic shift; the conventional associations of elegy and ode offer him the possibility of being coherent while yet remaining faithful to the inherently paradoxical nature of his theme. The traditional pastoral elegy speaks of a personal loss which is ultimately resolved by reference to some principle of order that places the loss in a universal perspective. In the *Ode*, Wordsworth's loss of the visionary gleam, begun as a pastoral elegy, is resolved in the intervening "ode" by recognition of just such a universal spiritual truth—that nature yet remembers what was so fugitive. Having stated the problem and asked its meaning, his speaker assumes a bardic voice and tells a story, a myth in fact, of the soul's journey, fall, and survival. This remains, however, a myth still grounded in individual experience, even as the poet's rhetoric implies revealed truth in the myth, an authority by which one traditionally expected the bard to speak.

There is a second, and possibly more speculative, significance in this generic modulation. The shift from "elegy" to "ode" coincides with the point at which Wordsworth suspended composition for two years—after stanza 4. Whatever biographical data may be relevant to this pause—or impasse—his choosing to resume the poem in a new voice is at least congruent with the thematic development signaled by the generic shift, for it suggests that the initial question was unanswerable in the terms in which it had been asked. The new "prophetic voice" was not only desirable, therefore, but became a psychological and poetic necessity. Accordingly, Wordsworth chose, upon publication of the first edition of the *Ode*, an epigraph from Virgil, *Paulo majora canamus:* "Let us sing of somewhat greater things."

The final stanzas of the *Intimations Ode* show the reemergence of the "I", but without deserting the earlier "we": "The thought of *our* past years in *me* doth breed / Perpetual benediction" (emphasis mine). And so Wordsworth proceeds to celebrate that truth now known because learned through pain, concerning the true allegiance to the supreme human imagination and its triumphant marriage to the natural world. Nature, he sees, is a necessary participant in this consummation. Before the turning point, the Ode describes two states of human development, when first mind, and then nature, is dominant; but the third and last state entails a balance between the first two, or as Wordsworth elsewhere calls it, a marriage. Earth as the dominant force appears earlier as a female principle, showing figurative aspects that Wordsworth attributes to her elsewhere: nurse and foster mother. The unobtrusive personification immediately after the elegiac turn, in the phrase "nature yet remembers," subtly continues this metaphorical strategy. It is Wordsworth who remembers, of course, but nature provides the motive and impetus to remember; mind and nature are involved in a relationship almost impossible to disentangle: a union.

Hence there is the implicit third metaphor of nature as bride. Reexamination of the poem shows that this figure has been carefully anticipated. In stanzas 1 to 4, the natural world prepares for a festival, which may well be a wedding. It is a springtime holiday, "all the earth is gay,"

> While Earth herself is adorning,
> This sweet May-morning.

Children are gathering flowers "In a thousand valleys far and wide." But the speaker, though he concedes that "My head hath its coronal," does not perceive the significance of this wreath. He feels, one infers, like the ungracious wedding guest in the biblical parable who was bidden to the wedding feast and refused to go. He has the grace to feel ashamed of his inadequacy ("oh evil day, if I were sullen"), but he is unable to join in the celebration, not knowing that *he* is the anointed bridegroom.

Later, in stanza 7, as Wordsworth describes the child's education in the ways of the world, the image of the wedding recurs; the child "shapes," indiscriminately, some "fragment from his dream of human life,"

> A wedding or a festival,
> A mourning or a funeral.

(At this point one recalls that the poem's opening was both.) He toys with each activity thoughtlessly, heartlessly; these "dialogues of business, love, or strife" are not the true and fructifying exchange between mind and nature which is creative, and which also preserves freedom from nature's prison.

But stanzas 10 and 11, significantly, return to the opening

scene. The speaker has now joined the festival in spirit and in truth, by means of "thought" and imagination which have restored the original dominance of mind over nature, temporarily lost. His final apostrophe to nature is a love song, an epithalamion, fittingly:

> And O ye Fountains, Meadows, Hills and Groves,
> Forebode not any severing of our loves!

In a tone far more assured than in *Tintern Abbey* Wordsworth expresses hope for a future that threatens no divorce, no widowhood. He anticipates a quiet marriage to nature, lived "beneath [its] more habitual sway."

Most important to the resolution of the poem is Wordsworth's demonstration that this marriage is a creative relationship: "The clouds that gather round the setting sun / Do take a sober colouring from an eye / That hath kept watch o'er man's mortality," he says, and adds, "To me the meanest flower that blows can give / Thoughts that do often lie too deep for tears." The equality between partners is emphatic: both mind and nature give, both receive. The earlier broodings upon mortality, the fosterings of nature, have finally led to this consummation, to this paradise regained (Wordsworth's version of the Miltonic "paradise within"). The *Ode*'s conclusion describes that paradise which the mind, "when wedded to this goodly universe / In love and holy passion," shall find "A simple produce of the common day."[9] The apparently doomed youth who saw the visionary gleam fade was left with this "light of common day"; he had gradually become the redeemed man, who finds in that very loss a new heaven and a new earth.

I repeat, then, a note sounded earlier. To recognize that Wordsworth's ode embodies, consciously and pointedly, a structural pattern common to *Paradise Lost,* and manifest at the psychological, stylistic, and generic levels of the poem, is to see its often alleged disunity in quite a new context. Disunified it may be in one sense—as a piece of music might be termed disunified which began in soft minor strains and ended in triumphant major harmonies of another key. But the shift or modulation, however surprising it might seem at first reading, is nevertheless deliberate, even necessary. For the great biblical and Miltonic myth, which seemed to Wordsworth congruent with the history of his own and every man's spiritual development, contained as the essence of its shape this transformation from one mode to another—from E minor to C major, from the loss of the visionary gleam to the birth of "the philosophic mind." This is one instance in which, as Coleridge put it when speaking of organic form, the substance of a work could only grow by its own principles, "shaping itself from within." If the resolution of the *Ode* has puzzled some readers, it must be at least in part because they have failed to recognize the poem's shape and the region "whence it came."

Milton, in word and deed, provides a supreme model for the poet who matures from the merely personal lyric, through experience, into "something like prophetic strain" (of the three allusions to Milton in Dorothy's journals, two mention Wordsworth's reading "Il Penseroso"). As we have seen, this is the pattern of growth which Wordsworth has so pointedly enacted in this *Ode*.

Unfallen Adam in the garden might be seen as the prototype, not only of man but also of the Wordsworthian lyric pastoral poet whose perceptions overflow into expression. According to legend, speech was simple and uncomplicated in Eden, perception and expression virtually the same. As the animals were led before Adam for the first time, he named them, "as it were from a fountaine of prophesie."[10] But when innocence is gone, the gleam fled, Eden lost, Adam and the Wordsworthian lyric poet must then perceive and speak in a different mode, one which reflects that experience of loss, and yet bespeaks a wider world, a higher reality. Michael speaks to fallen Adam shortly before his departure into the fallen world:

> . . . only add
> Deeds to thy knowledge answerable, add Faith,
> Add Virtue, Patience, Temperance, add Love
> By name to come called Charity, the soul
> Of all the rest; then wilt thou not be loath
> To leave this Paradise, but shall possess
> A paradise within thee, happier far.   (XII, 581–87)

Virtue, patience, temperance, love—these are moral qualities, and in Michael's list all the words but Faith concern man's relation with his fellow man. Eden was isolated compared with the

world to come, as the elegy is private compared with the epic—
or the ode. The paradise the angel describes to Adam is clearly
akin to Wordsworth's "humanised" imagination which must concern itself with greater things—man, nature, and human life.

The characteristic quality of the unfallen state for Wordsworth
is joy, akin to Adam's paradisal bliss; in the fallen state it is
"strength," which is associated, like the fallen Adam's fortitude,
with power, knowledge, and new freedom. The poet of such
powers, writes Wordsworth,

> . . . oft
> Must turn elsewhere—to travel near the tribes
> And fellowships of men, and see ill sights
> Of madding passions mutually inflamed;
> Must hear humanity in fields and groves
> Pipe solitary anguish. . . .[11]

Wordsworth, in his later poetry, did turn more and more to
"greater things," to broader canvasses of human life and suffering which he sought to express in the voice of the bard. *The
Excursion* shows his adherence to the vow, *Paulo majora canamus.*
But the voice finally faltered into silence, and *The Recluse* was
never completed. Thus the *Intimation Ode* is tragic as *Paradise
Lost* is tragic; nothing can bring back the hour of splendor in
the grass. But within the bounds of the poem, for the moment
recorded there, the perilous transformation from personal to
prophetic seemed complete, and the loss itself another Fortunate
Fall.

Epilogue

With the *Intimations Ode*, this study reaches its somewhat arbitrary end; the slow transformation I have been tracing, however, was in no sense complete by 1804. But by then the experiential perspectives of other genres had largely been accommodated to the lyric mode. And the originally defining character of the "greater lyric" had been transformed, its public declamation of prayer and praise now expressed and validated in terms of the private experience of one lyric speaker.

It has not been part of my argument here to imply that *any* representative eighteenth-century poem belongs, demonstrably and by some historical necessity, to the lyric mode. For of course not every poem of that century can readily be seen as having participated in creating the important tradition I am examining. I have argued that perhaps the best working definition of the lyric mode I can propose is that of a work which "represents from within the virtual experience of a more or less particularized consciousness." The practical test for a critic is to establish that the work contain elements or salient properties which when understood in relation to that purpose seem to render the work, as an artistic whole, *most* fully intelligible. The test also entails that as many of the less salient features as possible be shown as functional in relation to that definitive lyric principle. This necessarily means that although one might perceive lyrical elements in any poem, or indeed in any work of literature (from *The Dunciad* to *Mrs. Dalloway*), a critical decision to term that work "a lyric" will depend upon the relative importance of the principle of "structure-by-revelation-of-individual-consciousness" in relation to rival structural principles which may disclose themselves. Thus lyricism is a matter of degree, and the exact point at which lyrical elements are deemed sufficiently definitive of the work's primary mode so that one will wish to call it a lyric, may prove problematic in some cases. (Might one, for example, want to regard Faulkner's *Absalom, Absalom* as constituting, in part, a vast prose lyric, or does the copresent narrative principle make it merely a highly lyrical novel?)

Secondly, my argument must not be taken to imply that a work's putative status as a lyric can constitute, or necessarily lead to, the only interesting truths about it, any more than the anthropologist's decision that a particular fossil is that of an early form of man can exhaust the questions he will want to ask about it—classification is only the beginning and never the end of analysis. Good genre criticism, I believe, is not a process of labeling but rather a variety of what Wittgenstein called "seeing as": it invites the reader to see the particular work as something, while yet knowing that this cannot prevent another from seeing it also, or alternatively, as something else. The early man now embodied in a fossil is also a particular compound of physical substances; moreover, he was once a hunter, food-gatherer, late-evolving primate, and perhaps founder or last survivor of a tribe or a race. For certain analytic purposes, some of these ways of seeing what he is or was may take priority over others, and some may prove quite useless.

In this study my main purpose is to see the masterpieces of eighteenth-century English poetry with a wholeness of vision, yet an attentiveness to component texture and detail. Perhaps, to venture a metaphor from chemistry, I might claim that I have brought out better than others have, the process by which the lyric mode is seen to have precipitated out of a solution where it had always been present, thus profoundly changing the predominant color and flavor of the ever-changing mixture which is our poetic tradition. If such a perspective reveals the mixture as such, and so avoids the traditional analytic procedure which sifts out component strains for labeling, one or two at a time, then the enterprise has to that extent succeeded. It might, in addition, encourage others to see if they can determine just how the composition of that mixture was to change in the two succeeding centuries, or in those that preceded. For other literary periods, perhaps, some other strain than the lyric might be a more suitable standard of reference. Some, of course, may decide that our poetic tradition is not a mixture at all, and prefer to see it as something quite different, with the result that they will discuss the works under examination here in quite different terms—as the literary consequence of a scientific empiricism in the ascendant, or of the popularity of an Ignatian meditative tradition; or as the recording of new poetic ways of looking at physical nature. Of my own chosen perspective I claim only that it is compelling, unaccountably neglected in the scholarly tradition, and quite as revealing as its rivals in helping us to see and understand the transition from English Renaissance to Romantic poetry.

Appendix

Il Penseroso

Hence vain deluding joys,
    The brood of folly without father bred,
How little you bested,
    Or fill the fixed mind with all your toys;
Dwell in some idle brain,   5
    And fancies fond with gaudy shapes possess,
As thick and numberless
    As the gay motes that people the Sunbeams,
Or likest hovering dreams,
    The fickle Pensioners of *Morpheus'* train.   10
But hail thou Goddess, sage and holy,
Hail divinest Melancholy,
Whose Saintly visage is too bright
To hit the Sense of human sight;
And therefore to our weaker view,   15
O'erlaid with black, staid Wisdom's hue.
Black, but such as in esteem,
Prince *Memnon's* sister might beseem,
Or that Starr'd *Ethiop* Queen that strove
To set her beauty's praise above   20
The Sea Nymphs, and their powers offended.
Yet thou art higher far descended;
Thee bright-hair'd *Vesta* long of yore,
To solitary *Saturn* bore;
His daughter she (in *Saturn's* reign,   25
Such mixture was not held a stain).
Oft in glimmering Bow'rs and glades
He met her, and in secret shades
Of woody *Ida's* inmost grove,
While yet there was no fear of *Jove.*   30
Come pensive Nun, devout and pure,

Sober, steadfast, and demure,
All in a robe of darkest grain,
Flowing with majestic train,
And sable stole of *Cypress* Lawn,   35
Over thy decent shoulders drawn.
Come, but keep thy wonted state,
With ev'n step, and musing gait,
And looks commercing with the skies,
Thy rapt soul sitting in thine eyes: 40
There held in holy passion still,
Forget thyself to Marble, till
With a sad Leaden downward cast,
Thou fix them on the earth as fast.
And join with thee calm Peace and Quiet,   45
Spare Fast, that oft with gods doth diet,
And hears the Muses in a ring
Aye round above *Jove's* Altar sing.
And add to these retired Leisure,
That in trim Garden takes his pleasure;   50
But first, and chiefest, with thee bring
Him that yon soars on golden wing,
Guiding the fiery-wheeled throne,
The Cherub Contemplation;
And the mute Silence hist along,   55
'Less *Philomel* will deign a Song,
In her Sweetest, saddest plight,
Smoothing the rugged brow of night,
While *Cynthia* checks her Dragon yoke,
Gently o'er th' accustom'd Oak;   60
Sweet Bird that shunn'st the noise of folly,
Most musical, most melancholy!
Thee Chantress oft the Woods among,
I woo to hear thy Even-Song;
And missing thee, I walk unseen   65
On the dry smooth-shaven Green,
To behold the wand'ring Moon,
Riding near her highest noon,
Like one that had been led astray
Through the Heav'n's wide pathless way;   70
And oft, as if her head she bow'd,
Stooping through a fleecy cloud.
Oft on a Plat of rising ground,
I hear the far-off *Curfew* sound,

Over some wide-water'd shore,   75
Swinging slow with sullen roar;
Or if the Air will not permit,
Some still removed place will fit,
Where glowing Embers through the room
Teach light to counterfeit a gloom,   80
Far from all resort of mirth,
Save the Cricket on the hearth,
Or the Bellman's drowsy charm,
To bless the doors from nightly harm:
Or let my Lamp at midnight hour,   85
Be seen in some high lonely Tow'r,
Where I may oft outwatch the *Bear,*
With thrice great *Hermes,* or unsphere
The spirit of *Plato* to unfold
What Worlds, or what vast Regions hold   90
The immortal mind that hath forsook
Her mansion in this fleshly nook:
And of those *Daemons* that are found
In fire, air, flood, or underground,
Whose power hath a true consent   95
With Planet, or with Element.
Sometime let Gorgeous Tragedy
In Scepter'd Pall come sweeping by,
Presenting *Thebes,* or *Pelops'* line,
Or the tale of *Troy* divine,   100
Or what (though rare) of later age,
Ennobled hath the Buskin'd stage.
But, O sad Virgin, that thy power
Might raise *Musaeus* from his bower,
Or bid the soul of *Orpheus* sing   105
Such notes as, warbled to the string,
Drew Iron tears down *Pluto's* cheek,
And made Hell grant what Love did seek.
Or call up him that left half told
The story of *Cambuscan* bold,   110
Of *Camball,* and of *Algarsife,*
And who had *Canace* to wife,
That own'd the virtuous Ring and Glass,
And of the wondrous Horse of Brass,
On which the *Tartar* King did ride;   115
And if aught else great Bards beside
In sage and solemn tunes have sung,

Of.Tourneys and of Trophies hung,
Of Forests, and enchantments drear,
Where more is meant than meets the ear.   120
Thus night oft see me in thy pale career,
Till civil-suited Morn appear,
Not trickt and frounc't as she was wont
With the Attic Boy to hunt,
But kerchieft in a comely Cloud,   125
While rocking Winds are Piping loud,
Or usher'd with a shower still,
When the gust hath blown his fill,
Ending on the rustling Leaves,
With minute-drops from off the Eaves.   130
And When the Sun begins to fling
His flaring beams, me Goddess bring
To arched walks of twilight groves,
And shadows brown that *Sylvan* loves
Of Pine or monumental Oak,   135
Where the rude Axe with heaved stroke
Was never heard the Nymphs to daunt,
Or fright them from their hallow'd haunt.
There in close covert by some Brook,
Where no profaner eye may look,   140
Hide me from Day's garish eye,
While the Bee with Honied thigh,
That at her flow'ry work doth sing,
And the Waters murmuring
With such consort as they keep,   145
Entice the dewy-feather'd Sleep;
And let some strange mysterious dream
Wave at his Wings in Airy stream,
Of lively portraiture display'd
Softly on my eyelids laid.   150
And as I wake, sweet music breathe
Above, about, or underneath,
Sent by some spirit to mortals good,
Or th' unseen Genius of the Wood.
But let my due feet never fail   155
To walk the studious Cloister's pale,
And love the high embowed Roof,
With antic Pillars massy proof,
And storied Windows richly dight,
Casting a dim religious light.   160

There let the pealing Organ blow
To the full voic'd Choir below,
In Service high and Anthems clear,
As may with sweetness, through mine eyes.
Dissolve me into ecstasies,   165
And bring all Heav'n before mine eyes.
And may at last my weary age
Find out the peaceful hermitage,
The Hairy Gown and Mossy Cell,
Where I may sit and rightly spell   170
Of every Star that Heav'n doth shew
And every Herb that sips the dew;
Till old experience do attain
To something like Prophetic strain.
These pleasures *Melancholy* give,   175
And I with thee will choose to live.

The "Poems" of Gray's *Elegy*

"Meditation Among the Tombs"

The Curfew tolls the knell of parting day,
The lowing herd wind slowly o'er the lea,
The plowman homeward plods his weary way,
And leaves the world to darkness and to me.

Save that from yonder ivy-mantled tow'r
The mopeing owl does to the moon complain
Of such, as wand'ring near her secret bow'r,
Molest her ancient solitary reign.

Beneath those rugged elms, that yew-tree's shade,
Where heaves the turf in many a mould'ring heap,
Each in his narrow cell for ever laid,
The rude Forefathers of the hamlet sleep.

Far from the madding crowd's ignoble strife,
Their sober wishes never learn'd to stray;
Along the cool sequester'd vale of life
They kept the noiseless tenor of their way.

Yet ev'n these bones from insult to protect
Some frail memorial still erected nigh,
With uncouth rhimes and shapeless sculpture deck'd,
Implores the passing tribute of a sigh.

Their name, their years, spelt by th'unletter'd muse,
Their place of fame and elegy supply:
And many a holy text around she strews,
That teach the rustic moralist to die.

For who to dumb Forgetfulness a prey,
This pleasing anxious being e'er resign'd,
Left the warm precincts of the chearful day,
Nor cast one longing ling'ring look behind?

The Epitaph

HERE rests his head upon the lap of Earth
A Youth to Fortune and to Fame unknown,
Fair Science frown'd not on his humble birth,
And Melancholy mark'd him for her own.

Large was his bounty, and his soul sincere,
Heav'n did a recompence as largely send:
He gave to Mis'ry all he had, a tear,
He gain'd from Heav'n ('twas all he wish'd) a friend.

No farther seek his merits to disclose,
Or draw his frailties from their dread abode,
(There they alike in trembling hope repose)
The bosom of his Father and his God.

"On the Universal Human Desire for Earthly Memorials"

Now fades the glimmering landscape on the sight,
And all the air a solemn stillness holds,
Save where the beetle wheels his droning flight,
And drowsy tinklings lull the distant folds;

The boast of heraldry, the pomp of pow'r,
And all that beauty, all that wealth e'er gave,
Awaits alike th'inevitable hour.
The paths of glory lead but to the grave.

Nor you, ye Proud, impute to These the fault,
If Mem'ry o'er their Tomb no Trophies raise,
Where thro' the long-drawn isle and fretted vault
The pealing anthem swells the note of praise.

Can storied urn or animated bust
Back to its mansion call the fleeting breath?
Can Honour's voice provoke the silent dust,
Or Flatt'ry sooth the dull cold ear of Death?

Yet ev'n these bones from insult to protect
Some frail memorial still erected nigh,
With uncouth rhimes and shapeless sculpture deck'd,
Implores the passing tribute of a sigh.

Their name, their years, spelt by th'unletter'd muse,
The place of fame and elegy supply:
And many a holy text around she strews,
That teach the rustic moralist to die.

For who to dumb Forgetfulness a prey,
This pleasing anxious being e'er resign'd,
Left the warm precincts of the chearful day,
Nor cast one longing ling'ring look behind?

On some fond breast the parting soul relies,
Some pious drops the closing eye requires;
Ev'n from the tomb the voice of Nature cries,
Ev'n in our Ashes live their wonted Fires.

For thee, who mindful of th'unhonoured Dead
Dost in these lines their artless tale relate;

If chance, by lonely contemplation led,
Some kindred Spirit shall inquire thy fate,

Haply some hoary-headed Swain may say,

HERE rests his head upon the lap of Earth
A Youth to Fortune and to Fame unknown,
Fair Science frown'd not on his humble birth,
And Melancholy mark'd him for her own.

Large was his bounty, and his soul sincere,
Heav'n did a recompence as largely send:
He gave to Mis'ry all he had, a tear,
He gain'd from Heav'n ('twas all he wish'd) a friend.

No farther seek his merits to disclose,
Or draw his frailties from their dread abode,
(There they alike in trembling hope repose)
The bosom of his Father and his God.

"Elegy"

The Curfew tolls the knell of parting day,
The lowing herd wind slowly o'er the lea,
The plowman homeward plods his weary way,
And leaves the world to darkness and to me.

Beneath those rugged elms, that yew-tree's shade,
Where heaves the turf in many a mould'ring heap,
Each in his narrow cell for ever laid,
The rude Forefathers of the hamlet sleep.

The breezy call of incense-breathing Morn,
The swallow twitt'ring from the straw-built shed,
The cock's shrill clarion, or the ecchoing horn,
No more shall rouse them from their lowly bed.

For them no more the blazing hearth shall burn,
Or busy housewife ply her evening care:
No children run to lisp their sire's return,
Or climb his knees the envied kiss to share.

Oft did the harvest to their sickle yield,
Their furrow oft the stubborn glebe has broke;
How jocund did they drive their team afield!
How bow'd the woods beneath their sturdy stroke!

Let not Ambition mock their useful toil,
Their homely joys, and destiny obscure;

Nor Grandeur hear with a disdainful smile,
The short and simple annals of the poor.

Perhaps in this neglected spot is laid
Some heart once pregnant with celestial fire,
Hands, that the rod of empire might have sway'd,
Or wak'd to extasy the living lyre.

But Knowledge to their eyes her ample page
Rich with the spoils of time did ne'er unroll;
Chill Penury repress'd their noble rage,
And froze the genial current of the soul.

Full many a gem of purest ray serene,
The dark unfathom'd caves of ocean bear:
Full many a flower is born to blush unseen,
And waste its sweetness on the desert air.

Some village-Hampden that with dauntless breast
The little Tyrant of his fields withstood;
Some mute inglorious Milton here may rest,
Some Cromwell guiltless of his country's blood.

Th'applause of list'ning senates to command,
The threats of pain and ruin to despise,
To scatter plenty o'er a smiling land,
And read their hist'ry in a nation's eyes

Their lot forbad: nor circumscrib'd alone
Their growing virtues, but their crimes confin'd;
Forbad to wade through slaughter to a throne,
And shut the gates of mercy on mankind,

The struggling pangs of conscious truth to hide,
To quench the blushes of ingenuous shame,
Or heap the shrine of Luxury and Pride
With incense kindled at the Muse's flame.

Yet ev'n these bones from insult to protect
Some frail memorial still erected nigh,
With uncouth rhimes and shapeless sculpture deck'd,
Implores the passing tribute of a sigh.

For thee, who mindful of th'unhonour'd Dead
Dost in these lines their artless tale relate;
If chance, by lonely contemplation led,
Some kindred Spirit shall inquire thy fate,

Haply some hoary-headed Swain may say,
'Oft have we seen him at the peep of dawn

'Brushing with hasty steps the dews away
'To meet the sun upon the upland lawn.

'There at the foot of yonder nodding beech
'That wreathes its old fantastic roots so high,
'His listless length at noontide wou'd he stretch,
'And pore upon the brook that babbles by.

'Hard by yon wood, now smiling as in scorn,
'Mutt'ring his wayward fancies he wou'd rove,
'Now drooping, woeful wan, like one forlorn,
'Or craz'd with care, or cross'd in hopeless love.

'One morn I miss'd him on the custom'd hill,
'Along the heath and near his fav'rite tree;
'Another came; nor yet beside the rill,
'Nor up the lawn, nor at the wood was he,

'The next with dirges due in sad array
'Slow thro' the church-way path we saw him born[e].
'Approach and read (for thou can'st read) the lay,
'Grav'd on the stone beneath yon aged thorn.'

The Epitaph

HERE rests his head upon the lap of Earth
A Youth to Fortune and to Fame unknown,
Fair Science frown'd not on his humble birth,
And Melancholy mark'd him for her own.

Large was his bounty, and his soul sincere,
Heav'n did a recompence as largely send:
He gave to Mis'ry all he had, a tear,
He gain'd from Heav'n ('twas all he wish'd) a friend.

No farther seek his merits to disclose,
Or draw his frailties from their dread abode,
(There they alike in trembling hope repose)
The bosom of his Father and his God.

Notes

Chapter One

1. "Lyric," in *A Handbook to Literature*, ed. C. Hugh Holman, 4th ed. (Indianapolis: Bobbs-Merrill, 1980), pp. 252–53; M. H. Abrams, *A Glossary of Literary Terms*, 3d ed. (New York: Holt, Rinehart, and Winston, 1971), pp. 89–90; C. Day Lewis, *The Lyric Impulse* (Cambridge: Harvard University Press, 1965), p. 3.

2. *Aristotle: Selections*, trans. Philip Wheelwright (New York: Odyssey Press, 1951), p. 295.

3. See Norman Maclean, "From Action to Image: Theories of the Lyric in the Eighteenth Century," in *Critics and Criticism*, ed. R. S. Crane (Chicago: University of Chicago Press, 1952), pp. 409–10.

4. Norman Maclean, "Theory of Lyric Poetry in English from the Renaissance to Coleridge" (Ph.D. diss., University of Chicago, 1940), p. 5, quoted by James L. Kinneavy, *A Study of Three Contemporary Theories of Lyric Poetry* (Washington, D.C.: Catholic University Press, 1956), p. 1.

5. M. H. Abrams, *The Mirror and the Lamp* (New York: Oxford University Press, 1953, 1958), esp. pp. 84–88.

6. Paul Hernadi, *Beyond Genre: New Directions in Literary Classification* (Ithaca, N. Y.: Cornell University Press, 1972).

7. "Genre Theory, the Lyric, and *Erlebnis*," in *Discriminations: Further Concepts of Criticism* (New Haven: Yale University Press, 1970), p. 252.

8. Käte Hamburger, *The Logic of Literature*, 2d rev. ed., trans. Marilyn J. Rose (Bloomington: Indiana University Press, 1973): ". . . in the lyric it is the . . . need (of the subject) which finds its satisfaction in self-expression and the coming to a knowledge of the soul in this expression itself " (p. 234).

9. Ibid., p. 233.

10. Ibid., p. 234.

11. Ibid., p. 277.

12. More recent theorists of literature, including the various post-

structuralists, have begun to discuss the issue of genre. See, for example, Jonathan Culler, *Structuralist Poetics: Structuralism, Linguistics, and the Study of Literature* (Ithaca, N.Y.: Cornell University Press, 1976); or Tzvetan Todorov, "The Origin of Genres," *New Literary History* 8 (1976): 159–70.

13. Elder Olson, "The Lyric," *PMMLA* 1 (1969):62. The implications of Olson's approach have been worked out by Gémino H. Abad, *A Formal Approach to Lyric Poetry* (Quezon City, Philippines: University of the Philippines Press, 1978).

14. Olson, "The Lyric," p. 64.

15. Ibid., pp. 60–61.

16. For example, "The Ruined Cottage," "Childe Roland to the Dark Tower Came," "Michael," "The Last Ride Together," "The Death of the Hired Man."

17. "An Outline of Poetic Theory," in *Critics and Criticism*, p. 560.

18. Michael Polanyi, *The Tacit Dimension* (New York: Doubleday, Anchor Books, 1967).

19. My argument that lyric poetry need not be limited to simulated utterance is consistent with the work of recent experimenters who have written "lyric" poems using only symbols; see, for example, Richard Kostelanetz's "Tributes to Henry Ford," in *The Norton Introduction to Literature: Poetry,* ed. J. Paul Hunter (New York: W. W. Norton, 1973), p. 381; or Dorthi Charles's "Concrete Cat," in X. J. Kennedy, *Literature: An Introduction to Fiction, Poetry, and Drama,* 2d ed. (Boston: Little, Brown, 1979), p. 606.

20. Suzanne Langer, *Feeling and Form* (New York: Charles Scribner's Sons, 1953), p. 212.

21. "Natural" and "fictive" discourse are Barbara Herrnstein Smith's terms, explained in *On the Margins of Discourse: The Relation of Literature to Language* (Chicago: University of Chicago Press, 1978). This distinction is useful in discussion of the lyric and in understanding the strategies of the Romantics, especially Wordsworth. "Natural discourse," according to Smith, is "any utterance that can only be *represented* as occurring." When Wordsworth called a poem "Lines Composed a Few Miles Above Tintern Abbey on Revisiting the Banks of the Wye on a Tour, July 13, 1798," he was doing all he could in the title to create the illusion that this fictive discourse was in fact "natural" by anchoring it in this wealth of journalistic detail. And though we know he visited and revisited the spot, we can be sure that his utterance did not spontaneously emerge in iambic pentameter. This interest in appearing to dissolve the margins of discourse may also throw light on Wordsworth's

insistence that poetry uses "the language really spoken by men" and it may illuminate his somewhat inept discussion of the function of meter.

22. See, for example, "Literary Genres," in René Wellek and Austin Warren, *Theory of Literature*, 3d ed. (New York: Harcourt Brace and World, 1956), pp. 226–37.

23. Northrop Frye, *Anatomy of Criticism* (Princeton, N.J.: Princeton University Press, 1957), p. 247.

24. Ibid., pp. 249–50.

25. For a comparable view of the function of literary language in general, see Georges Poulet, "The Phenomenology of Reading," *New Literary History* 1 (1969):53–68. Poulet's account and mine resemble one another insofar as both emphasize a merging of the reader's consciousness with one inside the work, or, alternatively, a temporary displacement of the former by the latter. The important difference in context, however, is that he is speaking of the *authorial* consciousness which pervades any work, not just a lyric, whereas I am stressing the absorption by the reader of a lyric *speaker's* (fictive) consciousness: not an invariable experience of literature, but one peculiar to the lyric mode.

26. Consider, besides Poulet, Robert Langbaum, *The Poetry of Experience* (New York: Random House, 1957), pp. 24ff.

27. Wayne C. Booth, *The Rhetoric of Fiction* (Chicago: University of Chicago Press, 1961), pp. 73–74.

28. I wish to record my indebtedness to Professor Helen Vendler who taught me during my tenure as an NEH Fellow-in-Residence at Boston University (1977–78) that not all lyrics have a first-person speaker. My thinking about this typology of the lyric was also stimulated by two essays published in *Critical Inquiry:* Ralph Rader's "The Dramatic Monologue and Related Lyric Forms" 3, no. 1 (Autumn 1976):131–51, and Victor E. Vogt's "Narrative and Drama in the Lyric: Robert Frost's Strategic Withdrawal" 5, no. 3 (Spring 1979):529–51.

29. Leslie Fiedler, "Archetype and Signature," in *Myths and Motifs in Literature,* ed. David J. Burrows et al. (New York: The Free Press, 1973), p. 28.

30. For a thorough discussion of the relation of riddles to the strategies of the lyric, see Andrew Welsh, *The Roots of Lyric* (Princeton, N.J.: Princeton University Press, 1978).

31. For a contrasting view, see Rader, "The Dramatic Monologue."

32. See Dorrit Cohn, *Transparent Minds: Narrative Modes for Presenting Consciousness in Fiction* (Princeton, N.J.: Princeton University Press, 1978), esp. chap. 1, "Psycho-Narration," pp. 21–57.

33. John Stuart Mill, "What is Poetry?" in *Essays on Poetry by John*

Stuart Mill, ed. F. Parvin Sharpless (Columbia, S.C.: University of South Carolina Press, 1976), p. 12.

CHAPTER TWO

1. *The Poems of Alexander Pope,* ed. John Butt (New Haven: Yale University Press, 1939). All quotations from *Eloisa to Abelard* are taken from this edition.

2. Brendan O Hehir, "Virtue and Passion: The Dialectic of 'Eloisa to Abelard,'" in *Essential Articles for the Study of Alexander Pope,* 2d ed., Maynard Mack, ed. (Hamden, Conn.: Archon Books, 1968), pp. 333–52; Robert Langbaum, *The Poetry of Experience* (New York: Random House, 1959), p. 82; Rebecca Price Parkin, *The Poetic Workmanship of Alexander Pope* (Minneapolis: University of Minnesota Press, 1955), p. 73; Murray Krieger, "'Eloisa to Abelard': The Escape from Body or the Embrace of Body," *Eighteenth-Century Studies* 3 (Fall 1969):28–47; Stephen J. Ackerman, "The Vocation of Pope's Eloisa," *Studies in English Literature* 19 (Fall 1979):445–57. Ackerman argues that Eloisa experiences a process of Jungian "individuation," which implies a lyric consciousness, though he assumes, as I do not, that she reconciles herself within the context of religious orthodoxy.

3. *The Correspondence of Alexander Pope,* ed. George Sherburn (Oxford: Clarendon Press, 1956), p. 338.

4. See Henry Pettit, "Pope's 'Eloisa to Abelard': An Interpretation," in *Essential Articles,* pp. 320–32.

5. W. K. Wimsatt, "Imitation as Freedom: 1717–1798," in *Forms of Lyric: Selected Papers from the English Institute,* ed. Reuben A. Brower (New York: Columbia University Press, 1970), pp. 47–74.

6. See Reuben A. Brower, *Alexander Pope: The Poetry of Allusion* (Oxford: Clarendon Press, 1959); Hoyt Trowbridge, "Pope's *Eloisa* and the *Heroides* of Ovid," in *From Dryden to Jane Austen* (Albuquerque: University of New Mexico Press, 1977), pp. 135–53.

7. There is no full-length study of Pope's debt to Milton, a promising theme. Cleanth Brooks's famous essay, "The Case of Miss Arabella Fermor," in *The Well-Wrought Urn* (New York: Harcourt Brace and World, 1947) touches on the parallels between Pope's *Rape of the Lock* and *Paradise Lost;* Krieger speaks of affinities between *Paradise Lost* and *Eloisa to Abelard* in the essay cited above; Barbara K. Lewalski has addressed the topic more inclusively, though briefly, in "On Looking into Pope's Milton," *Etudes Anglaises* 27, no. 4 (October–December 1974), pp. 481–500.

8. The influence of Milton's diction on eighteenth-century poetry is so pervasive that one almost takes it for granted. "Il Penseroso" was especially evident in elegiac and "graveyard" poetry. For documentation

of the pervasiveness of Miltonic diction throughout the century, see R. D. Havens, *The Influence of Milton on English Poetry* (Cambridge: Harvard University Press, 1922). In his essay "The Methods of Description in Eighteenth- and Nineteenth-Century Poetry," Geoffrey Tillotson writes that in ll. 155–70 of *Eloisa to Abelard*, "the separate couplets come near to being lost in the rhythm of the larger unit. We note that the description is given in a single sentence, in the manner of *Paradise Lost*. It is as near as Pope comes to writing Miltonic blank verse." *Restoration and Eighteenth-Century Literature: Essays in Honor of Alan Dugald McKillop*, ed. Carroll Camden (Chicago: University of Chicago Press, 1963), p. 237.

9. Compare Eloisa's experiences in church, ll. 267–76, with the Penseroso's. Quotations from Milton taken from *John Milton: Complete Poems and Major Prose*, ed. Merritt Y. Hughes (Indianapolis: The Odyssey Press, 1957).

10. O Hehir, "Virtue and Passion."

11. For example, Donne essayed one heroic epistle on the subject of Sappho, and Michael Drayton wrote a great many poems in this genre. He, like Pope, imitates the Ovidian model using later historical characters, such as "Rosamund to King Henry."

12. Rosalie Littell Colie, *The Resources of Kind: Genre Theory in the Renaissance* (Berkeley: University of California Press, 1973), p. 3.

13. In *New Approaches to the Eighteenth Century: Selected Papers from the English Institute*, ed. John Philip Harth (New York: Columbia University Press, 1974), pp. 33–78.

14. This is M. H. Abrams's phrase, used in *The Mirror and the Lamp*, p. 58. Abrams is paraphrasing Kant.

CHAPTER THREE

1. Among those searching for an adequate name are Josephine Miles, *Eras and Modes in English Poetry* (Berkeley: University of California Press, 1957). She proposes the term "classical mode" for the works written between 1660 and 1700, and "sublime mode" for those between 1700 and 1770. See also Ralph Cohen, "The Augustan Mode in English Poetry," in *Studies in the Eighteenth Century*, ed. R. F. Brissenden (Toronto: University of Toronto Press, 1968), pp. 171–92.

2. R. S. Crane, "The Houhnynms, the Yahoos, and the History of Ideas," in *The Idea of the Humanities* (Chicago: University of Chicago Press, 1967), 2:261–82.

3. Lawrence Lipking, "Periods in the Arts: Sketches and Speculations," *New Literary History* 1 (1969):194.

4. This argument is not mine. The term "Silver Age" was coined by A. N. Whitehead in *Adventures of Ideas* (New York: Macmillan, 1933) and used by both Basil Willey in *The Eighteenth-Century Background* (New

York: Columbia University Press, 1941) and Ian Jack in *Augustan Satire* (Oxford: Clarendon Press, 1964), pp. 1–14. In *The Resources of Kind* Colie also assumes that the Renaissance lasted essentially until the death of Swift.

5. Donald Greene, "Augustinianism and Empiricism: A Note on Eighteenth-Century Intellectual History," *Eighteenth-Century Studies* 1 (1967):33–68.

6. J. Huizinga, *The Waning of the Middle Ages* (New York: Anchor Books, 1954).

7. Donald Greene, *The Age of Exuberance: Backgrounds to Eighteenth-Century English Literature* (New York: Random House, 1970).

8. Walter Jackson Bate, *The Burden of the Past and the English Poet* (Cambridge: Harvard University Press, Belknap Press, 1970).

9. Sir Philip Sidney, "An Apology for Poetry," in *Elizabethan Critical Essays*, ed. G. Gregory Smith (Oxford: Clarendon Press, 1904), 1:151.

10. Charles Gildon, *The Complete Art of Poetry* (London: Charles Rivington, 1713; Garland facsimile ed., 1970), 1:173.

11. Sir Thomas Pope Blount, *De Re Poetica* (London: 1694; Garland facsimile ed., 1974), p. 9. This interesting collection is itself an example of a genre Colie names as characteristic of the Renaissance—the collection from various sources of items related to a single topic (Colie, *Resources of Kind*, p. 16).

12. Blount, *De Re Poetica*, p. 12.

13. Ibid., p. 11.

14. *Critical Works of John Dennis*, ed. Edward Niles Hooker (Baltimore: Johns Hopkins University Press, 1939–43), "The Grounds of Criticism in Poetry," 1:329.

15. Blount, *De Re Poetica*, p. 13.

16. Dennis, "Grounds of Criticism," p. 328.

17. Sidney, "Apology," pp. 154–55.

18. Blount, *De Re Poetica*, p. 6.

19. Ibid., p. 8.

20. Ibid., p. 11.

21. Sidney, "Apology," p. 157.

22. Gildon, *Art of Poetry*, p. 51.

23. Joseph Trapp, *Lectures on Poetry Read in the Schools of Natural Philosophy* (1712), trans. from the Latin with additional notes (London: 1742; Garland facsimile ed., 1970), p. 27.

24. Dennis, "Grounds of Criticism," p. 328.

25. Sidney, "Apology," p. 158.

26. Trapp, *Lectures*, p. 17.

27. Sidney, "Apology," p. 159.

28. Dennis, "Grounds of Criticism," p. 336.

29. Percy Bysshe Shelley, "A Defense of Poetry," in *Shelley's Poetry and Prose*, Norton Critical Edition, ed. Donald H. Reiman and Sharon B. Powers (New York: W. W. Norton, 1977), pp. 507–8.

30. "The Prospectus," l. 55.

31. Sidney, "Apology," pp. 154–55.

32. Ibid., p. 158.

33. Ibid., pp. 166–67.

34. Barbara K. Lewalski, *Protestant Poetics and the Seventeenth-Century Religious Lyric* (Princeton, N.J.: Princeton University Press, 1979), p. ix.

35. John Calvin, *Commentarie on the Psalms*, trans. Arthur Golding (London, 1840).

36. Blount, *De Re Poetica*, p. 1.

37. Sir William Temple, "Of Poetry," in *Critical Essays of the Seventeenth Century*, ed. J. Spingarn (Oxford: Clarendon Press, 1908–9), 3:88.

38. Gildon, *Art of Poetry*, p. 173.

39. Trapp, *Lectures*, p. 202.

40. Ibid., p. 203.

41. Samuel Holt Monk, *The Sublime* (Ann Arbor: University of Michigan Press, 1960).

42. Temple, "Of Poetry," p. 292.

43. Trapp, *Lectures*, pp. 14, 16.

44. Blount, *De Re Poetica*, p. 25.

45. Richard Baxter, *Poetical Fragments* (London, 1681), p. A4.

46. Ibid.

47. Sir Richard Blackmore, "Preface to Prince Arthur," in Spingarn, *Essays*, 3:227.

48. Gildon, *Art of Poetry*, pp. 26, 29.

49. Lewalski, *Protestant Poetics*, p. 14. See also Charles H. and Katherine George, *The Protestant Mind of the English Reformation, 1570–1640* (Princeton, N.J.: Princeton University Press, 1960).

50. John Calvin, *Institutes of the Christian Religion*, ed. John T. McNeill, trans. Ford Lewis Battles (Philadelphia: The Westminster Press, 1960), XX, i, 1, p. 35.

51. Calvin, *Institutes*, I, xv, 4, p. 190.

52. Edward Topsell, *The Histories of Four-footed Beasts* (London, 1607; facsimile ed., ed. T. Muffler, New York: Da Capo Press, 1967).

53. The patristic tradition was much more suspicious than was Calvin of the senses as means to the knowledge of God. St. Augustine writes that "the beholding of oneness is not granted to that soul which wanders towards many objects and eagerly pursues mental beggary . . . [which] can only be avoided by keeping aloof from the multitude; and I mean, not just the multitude of men, but of all things that the senses reach."

De Ordine (*Divine Providence and the Problem of Evil*) (New York: Cosmopolitan Science and Art, 1942), p. 7.

54. John Calvin, *The Sermons of Maister John Calvin upon the Booke of Job*, trans. Arthur Golding (London, 1584).

55. Richard Baxter, *The Saints Everlasting Rest* (London, 1650), pp. 756–57.

56. Joseph Hall, *The Art of Divine Meditation*, 2d ed. (London: 1631).

57. Topsell, *Histories*, from the Epistle Dedicatory, A₃.

58. Thomas Goodwin, *The Vanity of Thoughts Discovered* (London: 1638), pp. 22, 8.

59. Edward Reynolds, *A Treatise on the Passions and Faculties of the Soule of Man, with the several Dignities and Corruptions thereunto Belonging* (London: 1640), p. 9.

60. Topsell, *Histories*, p. A₃.

61. Goodwin, *Vanity*, p. 12.

62. Louis L. Martz, *The Poetry of Meditation*, rev. ed. (New Haven: Yale University Press, 1962). Martz also applies his thesis concerning the influence of Jesuit meditational practice only to poetry before 1650, "a date that is not merely convenient, but is symptomatic of profound changes in English religious life. . . . It is the date of the appearance of Richard Baxter's *The Saints Everlasting Rest*" (p. 21).

63. Joseph Hall, *Occasional Meditations*, 2d ed. (London, 1631), from the Introduction.

64. Godfrey Goodman, *The Creatures Praysing God: or, The Religion of dumbe Creatures: an Example and Argument for the stirring up of our devotion and for the confusion of Atheism* (London, 1624).

65. Ibid., p. 16.

66. This is in Golding's translation into English.

67. Theodore Beza, *Job expounded* (London, 1589), from the Preface.

68. Calvin, *Job*, p. 675.

69. Humphreys, Richard, *Iob's Pietie, or, The patterne of the perfect man* (London, 1624); J. Manley, *The Affliction and Deliverance of the Saints; or, the Whole Book of Job* (London, 1652); [Jean François Senault] *The Pattern of Patience in the Example of the Holy Job* (London, 1651); Arthur Brett, *Patientia Victrix: or, The Book of Job Paraphras'd* (London, 1661); George Hutcheson, *An Exposition on the Book of Job. Being the sum of cccxvi lectures preached in the City of Edinburgh* (London, 1671); Joseph Caryl, *An Exposition with Practical Observations upon the . . . Chapters of Job*, 16 vols. (London, 1643–70).

70. Dr. Cobden, "On Dr. Young's Translation of Part of Job," in Alexander Chalmers, ed., *The Works of the English Poets from Chaucer* (London, 1810), 18:413.

71. Chalmers includes paraphrases of part of Job by William Broome,

Samuel Boyse, Christopher Pit, and Thomas Warton. Others published separately include W. Thompson, *A Poetical Paraphrase on part of the Book of Job in imitation of the style of Milton* (Dublin, 1726); *A Short Paraphrase on the Book of Job with Arguments to each Chapter by a Presbyter of the Church of England* (London, 1716); D. Bellamy, *A Paraphrase on the sacred history, or the Book of Job with observations from various authors* (London, 1748); *The Book of Job in Meeter . . . by R. P.,* Minister of the Gospel (London, n.d.); *The Complaint of Job: A Poem* (London, 1734); Daniel Baker, *The History of Job: A sacred poem in 6 books* (London, 1706); A gentleman, *Age in Distress: or Job's lamentation for his children. A Poem in blank verse* (London, 1750); Thomas Gent, *The Pattern of Piety: or tryals of patience. Being the most faithful spiritual songs of the life and death of the once afflicted Job* (Scarborough, 1734).

72. Edward Young, *The Complete Works,* James Nicols, ed. (facsimile of 1854 ed., Hildesheim: Georg Olms Verlagsbuchhandlung, 1968), 1, pp. 246–47.

73. Sir Richard Blackmore, *Paraphrase on Job* (London, 1700), from the Preface.

74. Young, *Works,* 1:259.

75. Dionysius Longinus, *On the Sublime,* trans. with notes and observations by William Smith, 3d ed. (London, 1752), p. 93.

76. Bishop Symon Patrick, author of a popular commentary on Job, describes the speech from the whirlwind as "taking up the Argument begun by Elihu (who came nearest to the truth) and prosecuting it in unimitable words (excelling his and all other men's . . .). He convinces Job of his Ignorance and Weakness."

77. William Perkins, *The Arte of Prophesying,* in *Workes,* vol. 2 (London, 1612–13).

78. Lewalski, *Protestant Poetics,* p. 31.

79. Marjorie H. Nicolson, *Mountain Gloom and Mountain Glory: The Development of the Aesthetics of the Infinite* (New York: W. W. Norton, 1963), p. 79.

80. Trapp, *Lectures,* p. 204.

81. Spingarn, *Essays,* 2:86.

82. Brett, *Patientia Victrix,* ll. 1–5.

83. Blount, *De Re Poetica,* p. 66.

84. Ibid., p. 67.

85. Ibid., pp. 67–68.

86. Ibid., p. 68.

87. Ibid.

88. Trapp, *Lectures,* p. 204.

89. Edward Young, "On Lyric Poetry," in *Eighteenth-Century Critical*

Essays, ed. Scott Elledge (Ithaca, N.Y.: Cornell University Press, 1961), 1:411–12.

90. Spingarn, *Essays,* 3:82.

91. Trapp, *Lectures,* p. 204.

92. Spingarn, *Essays,* 3:82.

CHAPTER FOUR

1. Martin Price, *To the Palace of Wisdom: Studies in Order and Energy from Dryden to Blake* (Garden City, N.Y.: Doubleday, 1964).

2. James Thomson, *The Seasons,* ed. James Sambrook (Oxford: Clarendon Press, 1981). All quotations are from this text.

3. Young, *Works,* 1:2.

4. Ibid., pp. 195, 197.

CHAPTER FIVE

1. Howard D. Weinbrot, *The Formal Strain: Studies in Augustan Imitation and Satire* (Chicago: University of Chicago Press, 1969); Walter Jackson Bate, "Johnson and Satire Manqué," in *Eighteenth-Century Studies in Honor of Donald F. Hyde,* ed. W. H. Bond (New York: The Grolier Club, 1970), pp. 145–60; Leopold Damrosch, Jr., *Samuel Johnson and the Tragic Sense* (Princeton, N.J.: Princeton University Press, 1972); Jack, *Augustan Satire,* p. 145; Lawrence Lipking, "Learning to Read Johnson: *The Vision of Theodore* and *The Vanity of Human Wishes,*" *English Literary History* 43 (Winter 1976):527–35; T. S. Eliot, "Johnson's 'London' and 'The Vanity of Human Wishes'," in *English Critical Essays: Twentieth Century,* ed. Phyllis M. Jones (London: Oxford University Press, 1933), pp. 301–9; one of the few essays arguing for the poem's "poetry" is Frederick W. Hilles's "Johnson's Poetic Fire," in *From Sensibility to Romanticism: Essays Presented to Frederick A. Pottle,* ed. Frederick W. Hilles and Harold Bloom (New York: Oxford University Press, 1965), pp. 67–77.

2. Damrosch, *Johnson,* p. 149.

3. *The Yale Edition of the Works of Samuel Johnson,* vol. 4, *Poems,* ed. E. L. McAdam with George Milne (New Haven: Yale University Press, 1964). All references are to this edition.

4. Harold Bloom, *The Anxiety of Influence: A Theory of Poetry* (New York: Oxford University Press, 1973), p. 14.

5. This sonnet has interesting affinities with Johnson's poem. It is remarkably impersonal for a sonnet; though it has a first-person speaker, he recounts not his own but another's purported experience. It is equally pessimistic, and finds grounds for this pessimism in the human "fear and hope / Which ever weave their shadows o'er the chasm." And he also explicitly aligns himself with Ecclesiastes, "the Preacher."

6. Robert Lowth, *Lectures on the Sacred Poetry of the Hebrews* (Garland facsimile ed., 1971; London, 1787), 2:14.

7. Ibid., p. 16.

8. Northrop Frye, *The Great Code: The Bible and Literature* (New York: Harcourt Brace Jovanovich, 1982), pp. 29–30.

9. *The Yale Edition of the Works of Samuel Johnson*, vol. 7, *Johnson on Shakespeare*, ed. Arthur Sherbo (New Haven: Yale University Press, 1968), p. 66.

10. For an exception, see Edward Bloom, "*The Vanity of Human Wishes:* Reason's Images," *Essays in Criticism* 15 (Spring 1965):181–92.

11. *Preface to Shakespeare*, p. 70.

12. Walter Jackson Bate, *Samuel Johnson* (New York: Harcourt Brace Jovanovich, 1975), p. 278.

13. Rachel Trickett, *The Honest Muse: A Study in Augustan Verse* (Oxford: Clarendon Press, 1967), pp. 245–46.

14. Frye, *Code*, p. 128.

CHAPTER SIX

1. Cleanth Brooks, *The Well-Wrought Urn* (New York: Harcourt Brace and World, 1947), pp. 96–113.

2. *The Complete Poems of Thomas Gray*, H. W. Starr and J. R. Hendrickson, eds. (Oxford: Clarendon Press, 1966), p. 40. All quotations are from this edition.

3. For a summary of opinions about the identity of the Youth, see Herbert W. Starr, "A Youth to Fortune and to Fame Unknown: A Reestimation," in *Twentieth-Century Interpretations of Gray's Elegy*, H. W. Starr, ed. (Englewood Cliffs, N.J.: Prentice-Hall, 1968), pp. 41–50.

4. Brooks, *Well-Wrought Urn*, p. 111. See also W. K. Wimsatt, "Imitation as Freedom," in *Forms of Lyric: Selected Papers from the English Institute*, ed. Reuben A. Brower (New York: Columbia University Press, 1970), p. 56ff.; Bertrand H. Bronson, "On a Special Decorum in Gray's 'Elegy,'" in *Facets of the Enlightenment: Studies in English Literature and Its Contexts* (Berkeley and Los Angeles: University of California Press, 1968), pp. 153–58.

5. S. T. Coleridge, *Biographia Literaria*, chap. 14.

6. I. A. Richards, *Practical Criticism: A Study of Literary Judgment* (New York: Harcourt Brace, 1939), p. 253.

7. A. E. Dyson, "The Ambivalence of Gray's 'Elegy,'" in Starr, *Twentieth-Century Interpretations*, pp. 83–87; William Rider, *An Historical and Critical Account of the Living Authors of Great Britain* (London, 1792).

8. Trapp, *Lectures*, p. 164.

9. Ibid., 165.

10. For Wordsworth, the moon is consistently a symbol of the Imag-

ination, as in the climbing of Snowdon or in the meeting of the discharged soldier in *The Prelude*. It has a similar symbolic significance in "The Rime of the Ancient Mariner," and "Frost at Midnight."

11. See, for example, Lyle Glazier, "Gray's 'Elegy': The Skull Beneath the Skin," in Starr, *Twentieth-Century Interpretations*, p. 35.

12. Northrop Frye, "Literature as Context: Milton's 'Lycidas'," in *Fables of Identity: Studies in Poetic Mythology* (New York: Harcourt Brace and World, 1963), p. 121.

13. This term is, of course, M. H. Abrams's in his important essay on the longer lyrics of the Romantics, "Structure and Style in the Greater Romantic Lyric," in Hilles and Bloom, *From Sensibility to Romanticism*, pp. 527–60.

14. See, for example, lines 42–44.

15. An equally intense concentration of Miltonic echoes appears in those lines where the speaker imagines the lives of the dead villagers.

CHAPTER SEVEN

1. *Collected Works of Oliver Goldsmith*, ed. Arthur Friedman (Oxford: Clarendon Press, 1966), p. 285.

2. John Scott, *Critical Essays*, in *Goldsmith: The Critical Heritage*, ed. G. S. Rousseau (London: Routledge and Kegan Paul, 1974), p. 94.

3. Richard J. Jaarsma speaks of "the intrusion of the I" and argues that it is "a technical device," in "Ethics in the Wasteland: Image and Structure in Goldsmith's *Deserted Village*," *Texas Studies in Literature and Language* 13 (Fall 1971): 455; Earl Miner speaks of "the Tory mind," in "The Making of *The Deserted Village*," *Huntington Library Quarterly* 22 (1958–59): 130; Robert Mahoney discusses the metaphorical force of "lyrical simplicity," in "Lyrical Antithesis: The Moral Style of *The Deserted Village*," *Ariel: A Review of International English Literature* 8 (1977): 46.

4. This is Wordsworth's description of his poems in the *Lyrical Ballads* (*Preface* of 1800).

5. Miner argues that *The Deserted Village* is a version of pastoral *elegy*. This essay is enlightening in its emphasis on the conventionality of Goldsmith's lament. I believe, however, that to read the poem as a version of pastoral in general (pastoral elegy being but one phase of a larger set of conventions) suggests answers to more questions raised by the poem, particularly as to why virtue and poetry must depart.

6. "A Discourse on Pastoral Poetry," in *The Poems of Alexander Pope*, ed. John Butt (a reduced version of the Twickenham Text) (New Haven: Yale University Press, 1963), pp. 119–21.

7. This personification also accounts for the somewhat odd reference to the "decent church" in the description. The older sense of "decent" is "decorous," and this is probably the one Goldsmith had in mind. But

"decent" was beginning to acquire its sexual connotations as well. (See the discussion of "bower," "swain," etc., below.)

8. Morris Golden, "The Broken Dream of *The Deserted Village*," *Literature and Psychology* 9 (Fall 1959):44.

9. Ibid., p. 46.

10. Goldsmith's language is conventional here as well. Compare ll. 90–93 from Pope's "Autumn: The Third Pastoral, or Hylas and AEgon":

> Wolves gave thee suck, and savage Tygers fed.
> Thou were from AEtna's burning Entrails torn,
> Got by fierce Whirlwinds, and inThunder born!

11. I emphatically wish to maintain the distinction between the historical Goldsmith and his speaker as a fictional construct. In light of my analysis of this speaker, however, it is fascinating to consider the plot of *She Stoops to Conquer*. The hero, Marlow, suffers from a condition a Freudian would identify as oedipal in origin. He is tongue-tied and fearful in the presence of "modest" women (of his own class), never having been "familiarly acquainted with [any] except [his] mother." But among females "of another class" he is, in his friend Hastings's words, "impudent enough of all conscience" (Act 1). His problem is solved, of course, when he falls in love with Kate, believing this daughter of the squire to be a barmaid (*Collected Works*, 5:129).

CHAPTER EIGHT

1. Lionel Trilling, "Wordsworth and the Iron Time," in *Twentieth-Century Views of Wordsworth*, M. H. Abrams, ed. (Englewood Cliffs, N. J.: Prentice-Hall, 1972), p. 64; emphasis mine.

2. Richard Sewall, *The Vision of Tragedy* (New Haven: Yale University Press, 1959), p. 47.

3. *The Borderers* (III, ll. 1539; 1543–44), in *The Poetical Works of William Wordsworth*, Ernest de Selincourt, ed. (Oxford, 1940), I, p. 188.

4. *Don Juan*, Canto III, Stanza ix.

5. All quotations from *The Ruined Cottage* are taken from *The Ruined Cottage and The Pedlar*, ed. James Butler (Ithaca: Cornell University Press, 1979).

6. *Natural Supernaturalism* (New York: W. W. Norton, 1971), pp. 88–94.

7. Jonathan Wordsworth, *The Music of Humanity: A Critical Study of Wordsworth's "Ruined Cottage"* (London: Thomas Nelson and Sons, 1969), pp. 151–52.

8. James H. Averill, *Wordsworth and the Poetry of Human Suffering* (Ithaca, N.Y.: Cornell University Press, 1980), pp. 116–41.

9. In the final version of *The Excursion*, Book I, Wordsworth added

that Margaret was "tender and deep in her excess of love" (l. 514), a possible "tragic flaw." Also, some readers have questioned her moral responsibility in her distracted care of her children, particularly of the infant who dies. This argument seems to me to be founded upon a misapprehension of fictional mode, to assume that the story of Margaret is essentially realistic and offers psychological consistency and insight into motivation. I shall argue, however, that her history is nearer to a purely symbolic narrative in which characters tend to be types.

10. For a characteristic expression of late eighteenth-century opinion (which recognizes the book's dramatic qualities but also its differences from Greek tragedy), see Lowth, *Lectures*, 2:345–435.

11. Frye, "Myth, Fiction, and Displacement," in *Fables of Identity*, pp. 21–38.

12. Frye, *Anatomy*, p. 34.

13. Here Wordsworth's landscape is Spenserian in its particularities that evoke generalities. Words such as "common" imply that the narrator is an Everyman. Wordsworth, of course, admired Spenser greatly, and his very early works such as the Salisbury Plain poems are even more clearly influenced by Spenser.

14. Frye, *Anatomy*, p. 214.

15. Ibid.

16. See Abrams, *Natural Supernaturalism*, pp. 37–45.

17. Frye, *Anatomy*, p. 213.

18. Here, as in other poems such as "Michael," Wordsworth gives dignity and weight to his commonplace characters by evoking the Bible. Nettles and adders are biblical figures for destruction, danger, and decay. Compare Proverbs 24:31: "And behold it was filled with nettles, and thorns covered the face thereof, and the stone wall was broken down"; or Isaiah 11:8: "The sucking child shall play over the hole of the asp, and the weaned child shall put his hand in the adder's den."

19. One may note the resemblance of this moment to the strange opening of a novel written decades later by another Wordsworthian sensibility. The narrator of George Eliot's *The Mill on the Floss*, "in love with [the] moistness" of a mill pond, implicitly begins (as Wordsworth ends) with an enunciation of the theme—redemptive wisdom through witnessing another's tragic history.

20. Frye, *Anatomy*, p. 208.

21. The word "shew" or "show" apparently had a special significance for Wordsworth. He uses it frequently to describe natural manifestations of particular importance. He may have had in mind the relatively unusual meaning of "show" as "a manifestation of divine power."

22. Dictated to Isabella Fenwick, 1843.

CHAPTER NINE

1. John Jones sees the poem as a "preparation for the defeat of imaginative monism," in *The Egotistical Sublime* (London: Chatto and Windus, 1954), p. 167; Florence G. Marsh calls it "fractured," in "Wordsworth's *Ode:* Obstinate Questionings," *Studies in Romanticism* 6 (1965):226; Cleanth Brooks writes that the conclusion is not as fully realized poetically as the earlier expression of loss, that it is "asserted rather than dramatized," in *The Well-Wrought Urn*, p. 148; David Perkins questions the success of the work's ethical conclusion, in *The Quest for Permanence* (Cambridge: Harvard University Press, 1959), p. 80; Alan Grob finds the poem set apart from the body of Wordsworth's work: "The *Ode* remains alone *sui generis* set apart in magnificent isolation," in *The Philosophic Mind* (Columbus, Ohio: Ohio State University Press, 1973), pp. 261–62.

2. This unfamiliar thesis rests on several familiar assumptions about the *Ode*. Harold Bloom has noted Milton's role as a "precursor," though he is thinking primarily of *Lycidas: A Map of Misreading* (New York: Oxford University Press, 1975); Brooks, Hirsch, and others have assumed as I do that the *Ode* concerns the development of imagination; that it is also about the poet and his poetry has long been recognized as well. Brooks, *The Well-Wrought Urn*, pp. 124–50; E. O. Hirsch, *Wordsworth and Schelling: A Typological Study of Romanticism* (New Haven: Yale University Press, 1960), pp. 177–78. My reading is also fundamentally indebted to M. H. Abrams's thesis in *Natural Supernaturalism*, that the Romantics "undertook . . . to save traditional concepts, schemes, and values which had been based on the relation of the Creator to his creature and creation, but to reformulate them within the prevailing two-term system of subject and object, ego and non-ego" (p. 13).

3. Lionel Trilling, "The Immortality Ode," in *The Liberal Imagination* (New York, 1940; reprint, New York: Charles Scribner's Sons, 1953), pp. 129–59.

4. The grammar as well as the substance of stanza 9 is notoriously puzzling, of course, and the Fenwick note, written decades after the *Ode*, has done little to clarify it. Without the note, I suggest, the passage would be less perplexing because the reader might more readily see the universal paradox of the fortunate fall in Wordsworth's language. The note, however, specifies and particularizes the reference so as to make it idiosyncratic—just what Wordsworth was apparently trying to avoid in the poem itself. In fact, Brooks was the first to emphasize the crucial paradoxes in the *Ode*. A careful reading of the note, however, does not contradict my thesis. The memory of the "fallings, vanishings" is gratifying because the experience of loss remembered is his best evidence of the previous state, when he "communed with all that I saw as something not apart from but inherent in, my own immaterial na-

ture." Like Eden, this state can only be known by contrast. The "fallings ..." are not identical with the power also called "the gleam," but the moments at which its true power could be most intensely felt and hence known.

5. William Wordsworth, *The Prelude: 1799, 1805, 1850,* ed. Jonathan Wordsworth, M. H. Abrams, Stephen Gill, Norton Critical Edition (New York: W. W. Norton, 1979). Quotations are from the 1850 text.

6. Trilling notes (*The Liberal Imagination,* p. 132) that this "Celestial Light" is perhaps similar to the light which is praised in the invocation to the third book of *Paradise Lost.*

7. Helen Vendler also alludes to the poetic development spurred by the loss of the gleam as a "fortunate fall," but does not pursue the Miltonic context of allusion, in her essay, "Lionel Trilling and the Immortality Ode," *Salmagundi* 41 (1978):664–86.

8. ". . . as great Passion only is the adequate Language of the greater poetry [epic, tragedy, the ode], so the greater poetry is the only adequate language of Religion." John Dennis, "The Grounds of Criticism in Poetry," 1:340. Norman Maclean emphasizes this public tradition of the eighteenth-century ode in his essay "From Action to Image: Theories of the Lyric in the Eighteenth Century," in *Critics and Criticism,* pp. 408–62.

9. "The Prospectus," ll. 53–55.

10. Edward Topsell, *Histories,* A$_3$.

11. "The Prospectus," ll. 72–77.

Index